HEROINES OF THE GOLDEN AGE!

A COLORING COLLECTION OF PUBLIC DOMAIN SUPER-WOMEN

POCKET BOOK!

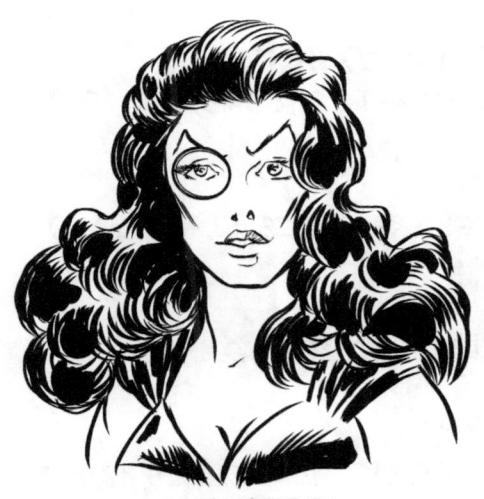

ILLUSTRATED BY
A. G. CEGLIA - L. LIVI

HEROINES OF THE GOLDEN AGE!
A COLORING COLLECTION OF PUBLIC DOMAIN SUPER-WOMEN
POCKET BOOK!

© 2019 LICORNE PRINTS (A BMS DIVISION).

LICORNE PRINTS
LICORNE@BEMYSTUDIO.COM

ALL ARTWORK © 2019 BLUE MONKEY STUDIO
ALL CHARACTERS TM AND © 2019 OF THEIR RESPECTIVE HOLDERS

THIS IS AN ACADEMIC WORK. THESE AND OTHER ©, ® AND TM APPEARS AS HISTORIC EXAMPLES FOR SCHOLARLY PURPOSES. ALL RIGHTS RESERVED. BLUE MONKEY STUDIO OR DODO PRINTS MAKE NO REPRESENTATION OF ANY RIGHTS TO SAID ©, ® AND TM.

ANY OMMISSION OR INCORRECT INFORMATION SHOULD BE TRANSMITTED TO THE AUTHOR OR THE PUBLISHER SO IT CAN BE RECTIFIED IN FUTURE EDITION OF THIS BOOK.

NO PART OF THIS BOOK MAY BE USED OR REPRODUCED IN ANY MANNER WHATSOEVER WITHOUT WRITTEN PERMISSION EXCEPT IN THE CASE OF BRIEF QUOTATIONS EMBODIED IN CRITICAL ARTICLES AND REVIEWS.

CHARACTER LIST

AMAZONA THE MIGHTY WOMAN
(FICTION HOUSE, PLANET COMICS #3, MAR. 1940)

BLACK ANGEL
(HILLMAN, AIR FIGHTERS COMICS #2, NOV. 1942)

BLACK CAT
(HARVEY, POCKET COMICS #1, AUG. 1941)

BLACK ORCHID
(HARVEY, ALL-NEW SHORT STORY COMICS #2, MAR. 1943)

BLACK ORCHID
(CONSOLIDATED, TOPS COMICS (UNNUMBERED), 1944)

BLACK VENUS
(HOLYOKE/AVIATION, CONTACT COMICS #1, JULY 1944)

BLACK WIDOW
(HOLYOKE, CAT-MAN COMICS #1, MAY 1941)

BLUE LADY
(CENTAUR, CCA, AMAZING-MAN COMICS #24, OCT. 1941)

CAROL PAIGE, BRAD SPENCER WONDERMAN'S GIRLFRIEND
(BETTER/NEDOR/STANDARD, COMPLETE BOOK OF COMICS AND FUNNIES #1, 1944)

DARA OF THE VIKINGS
(AVON, STRANGE WORLDS #2, SEPT. 1951)

DOMINO LADY
(FICTION HOUSE, SAUCY ROMANTIC ADVENTURES, MAY 1936)

FANTOMAH
(FICTION HOUSE, JUNGLE COMICS #2, FEB 1940)

FRAN FRAZER
(MLJ, TOP-NOTCH COMICS #9, OCT. 1940)

JILL TRENT
(BETTER/NEDOR/STANDARD, FIGHTING YANK #6, DEC. 1943)

KITTEN, CATMAN'S SIDEKICK
(HOLYOKE, CAT-MAN COMICS #5, DEC. 1941)

KITTY KELLY
(HARRY "A" CHESLER, PUNCH COMICS #1, DEC. 1941)

LADY FAIRPLAY
(PROGRESSIVE, BANG-UP COMICS #1, DEC. 1941)

LADY LUCK
(QUALITY, SMASH COMICS #42, APR. 1943)

LADY SATAN
(HARRY "A" CHESLER, DYNAMIC COMICS #2, DEC. 1941)

LADY SERPENT
(BETTER/NEDOR/STANDARD, THE BLACK TERROR #23, JUNE. 1948)

LADY TARNA
(BETTER/NEDOR/STANDARD, COMPLETE BOOK OF COMICS AND FUNNIES #1, 1944)

MADAM SATAN*
(ARCHIE/MLJ, PEP COMICS #16, JUNE 1941)

MADAME STRANGE
(GREAT, GREAT COMICS #1, NOV. 1941)

MISS MASQUE
(BETTER/NEDOR/STANDARD, EXCITING COMICS #51, SEPT. 1946)

MISS VICTORY
(HOLYOKE, CAPTAIN FEARLESS COMICS #1, AUG. 1941)

MOON GIRL*
(EC, THE HAPPY HOULIHANS #1, FALL 1947)

MOTHER HUBBARD
(HARRY "A" CHESLER, SCOOP COMICS #1, NOV. 1941)

NELVANA OF THE NORTHERN LIGHTS*
(HILLBOROUGH, TRIUMPH-ADVENTURE-COMICS #1, AUG. 1941)

PHANTOM LADY I
(FOX FEATURE, ALL-TOP COMICS #8, NOV. 1947)

PHANTOM LADY II
(AJAX-FARRELL, PHANTOM LADY #1, DEC. 1944/JAN. 1955)

QUEEN MERMA, BARRICUDA'S GIRLFRIEND
(HARRY "A" CHESLER, YANKEE COMICS #2, NOV. 1941)

RED ANN
(BETTER/NEDOR/STANDARD, THE BLACK TERROR #24, SEPT. 1948)

ROCKET GIRL
(HARRY "A" CHESLER, SCOOP COMICS #1, NOV. 1941)

SPIDER QUEEN
(FOX FEATURE, THE EAGLE #2, SEPT. 1941)

SPIDER WOMAN
(HARRY "A" CHESLER, MAJOR VICTORY COMICS #1, 1944)

USA
(QUALITY, FEATURE COMICS #42, MAR. 1941)

VEILED AVENGER
(HARRY "A" CHESLER, SPOTLIGHT COMICS #1, NOV. 1944)

WAR NURSE
(HARVEY, SPEED COMICS #13, MAY 1941)

WILDFIRE
(QUALITY, SMASH COMICS #25, AUG. 1941)

WOMAN IN RED
(BETTER/NEDOR/STANDARD, THRILLING COMICS #2, MAR. 1940)

YANKEE GIRL
(HARRY "A" CHESLER, DYNAMIC COMICS #23, 1947)

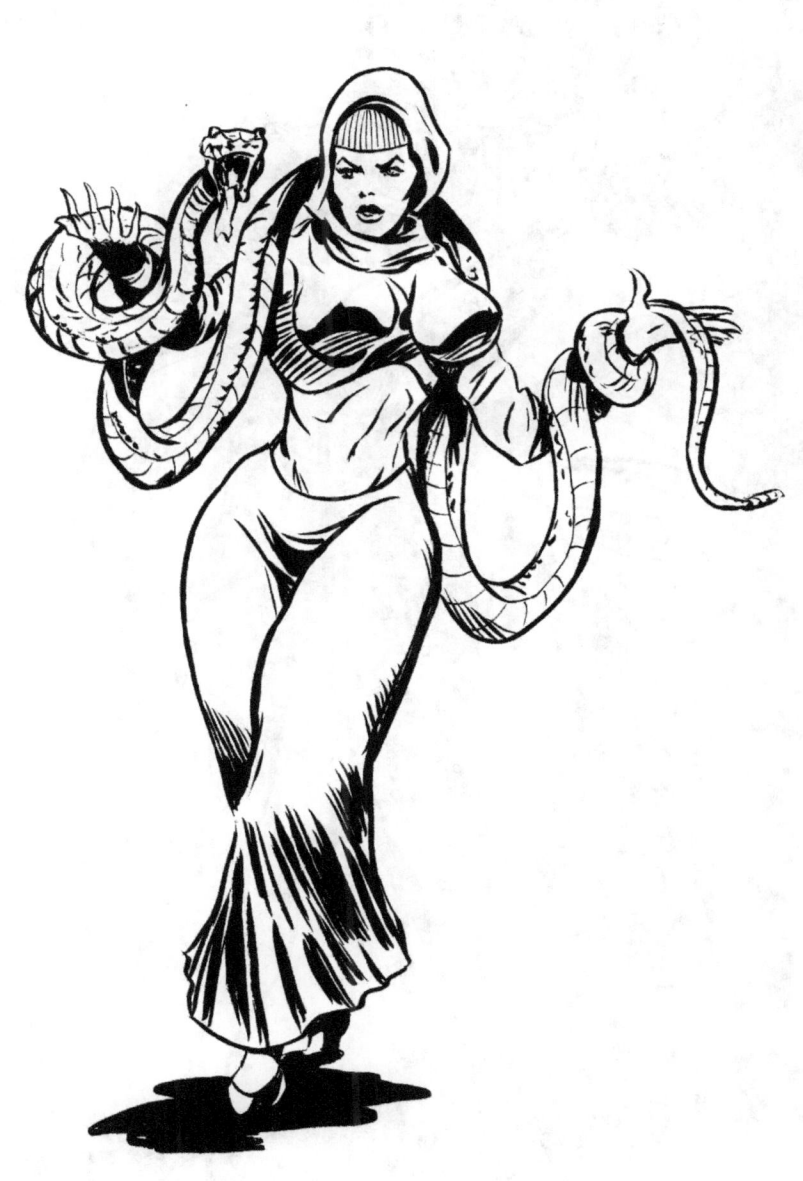

LADY SERPENT - NEDOR

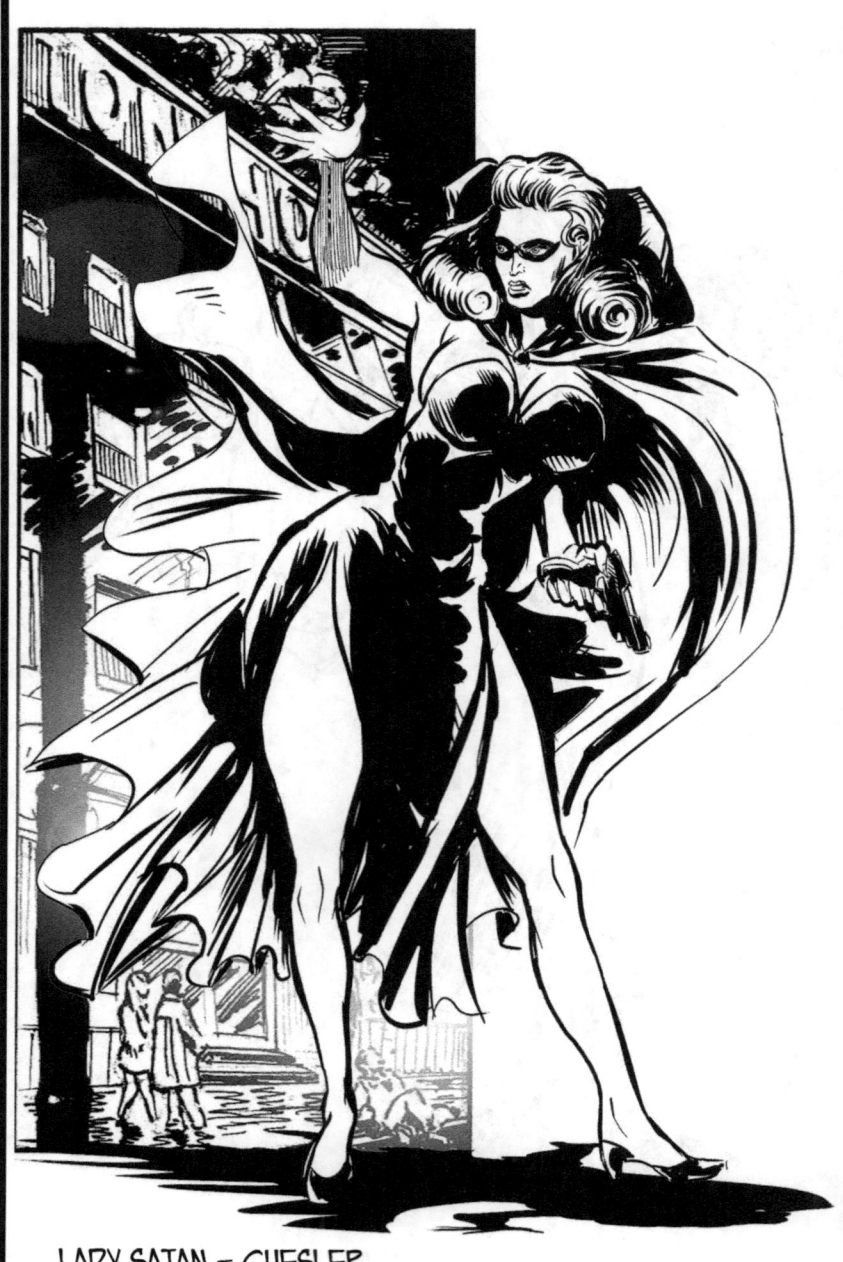

LADY SATAN - CHESLER

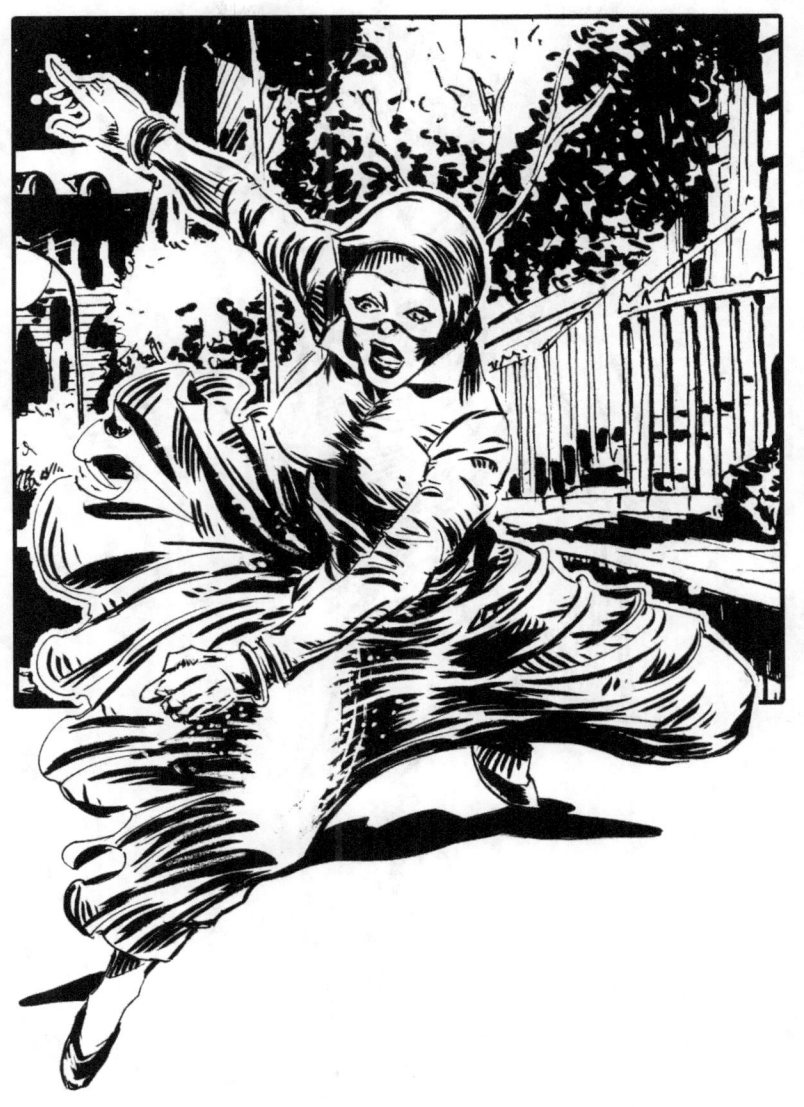

WOMAN IN RED - NEDOR

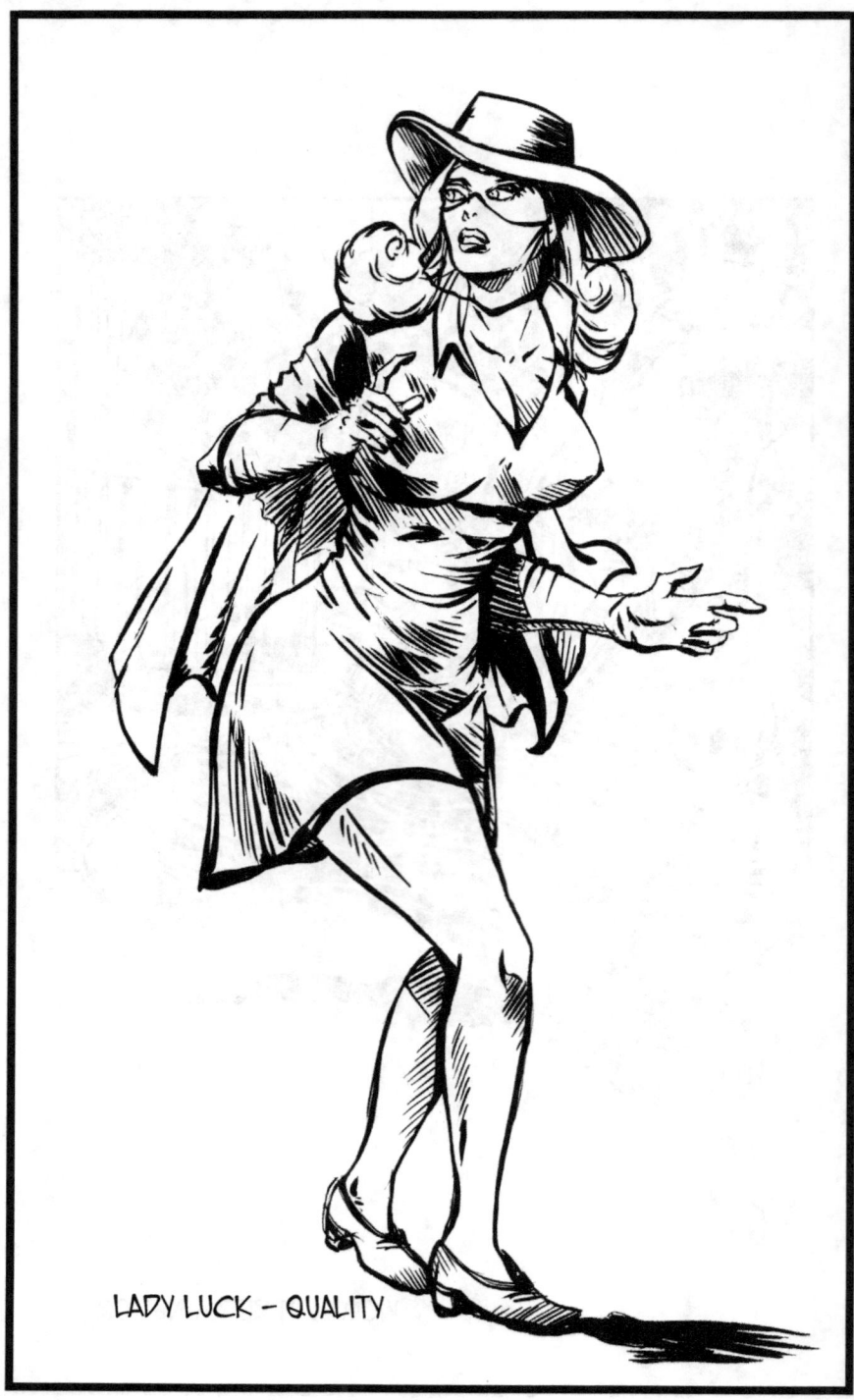

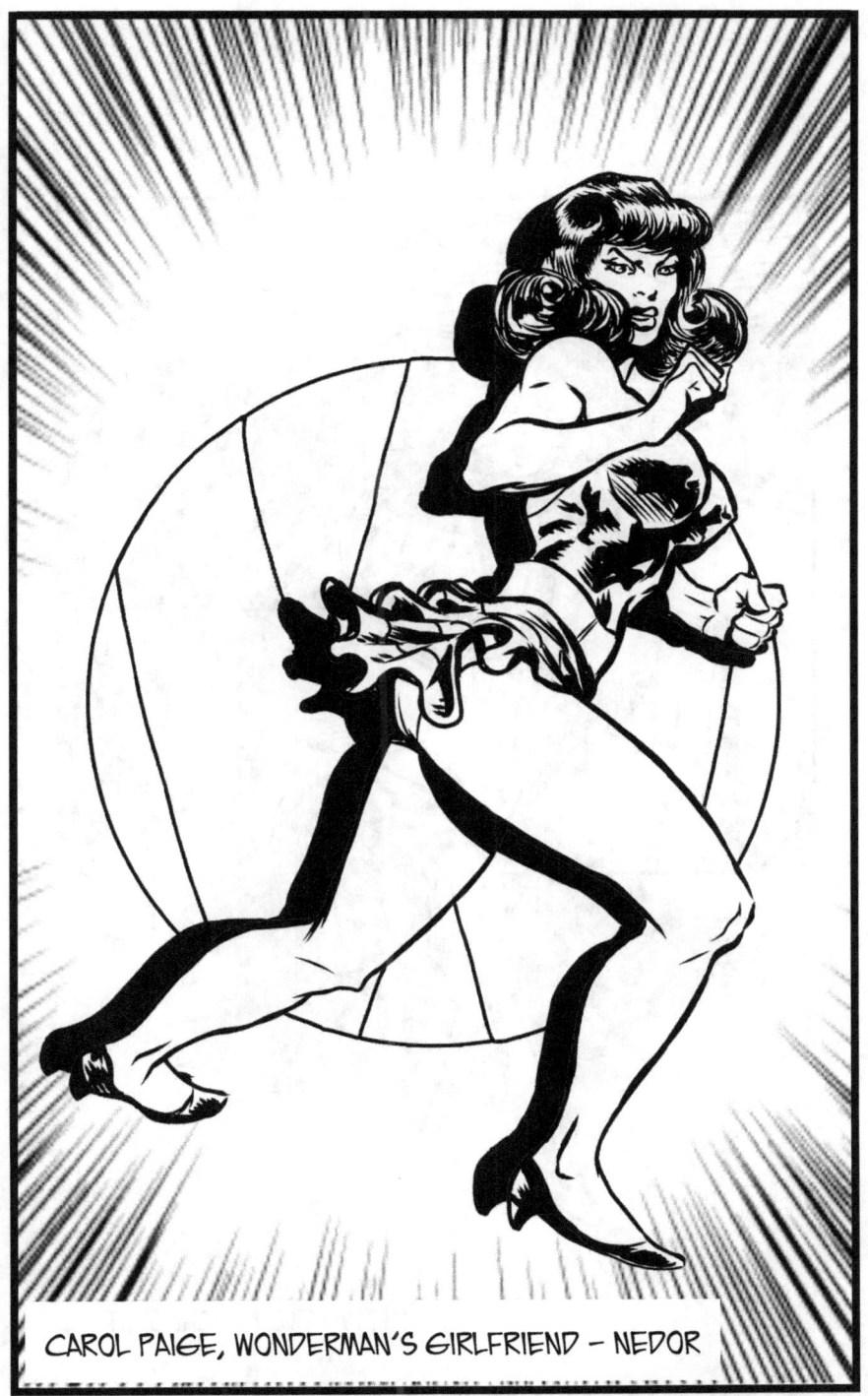

CAROL PAIGE, WONDERMAN'S GIRLFRIEND - NEDOR

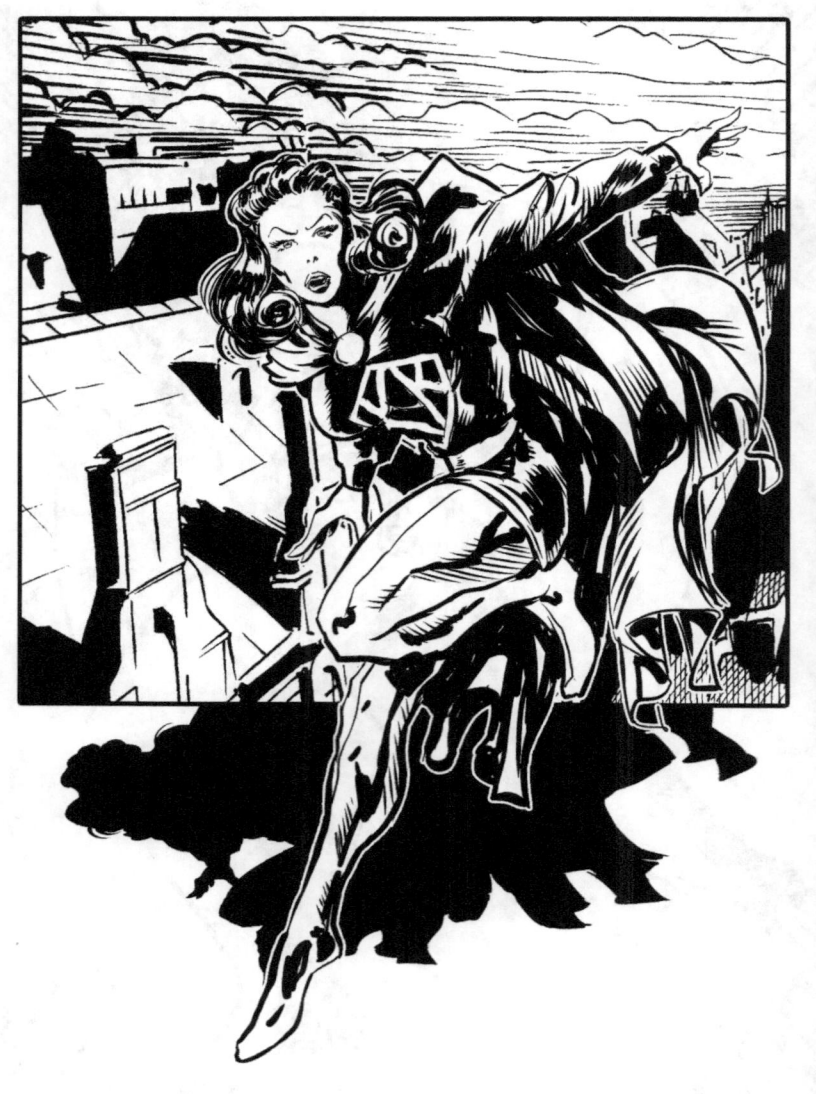

KITTY KELLY - CHESLER

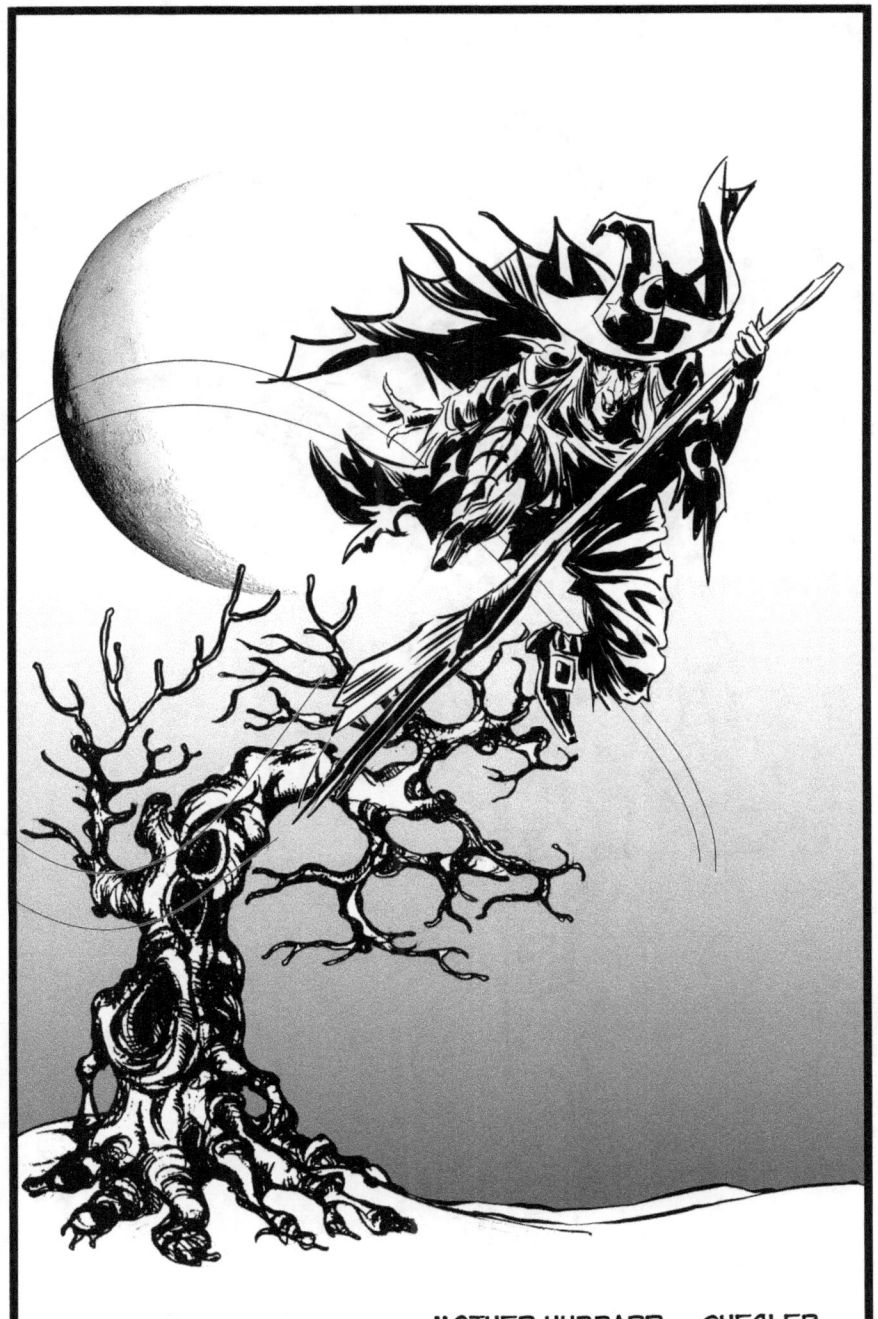

MOTHER HUBBARD – CHESLER

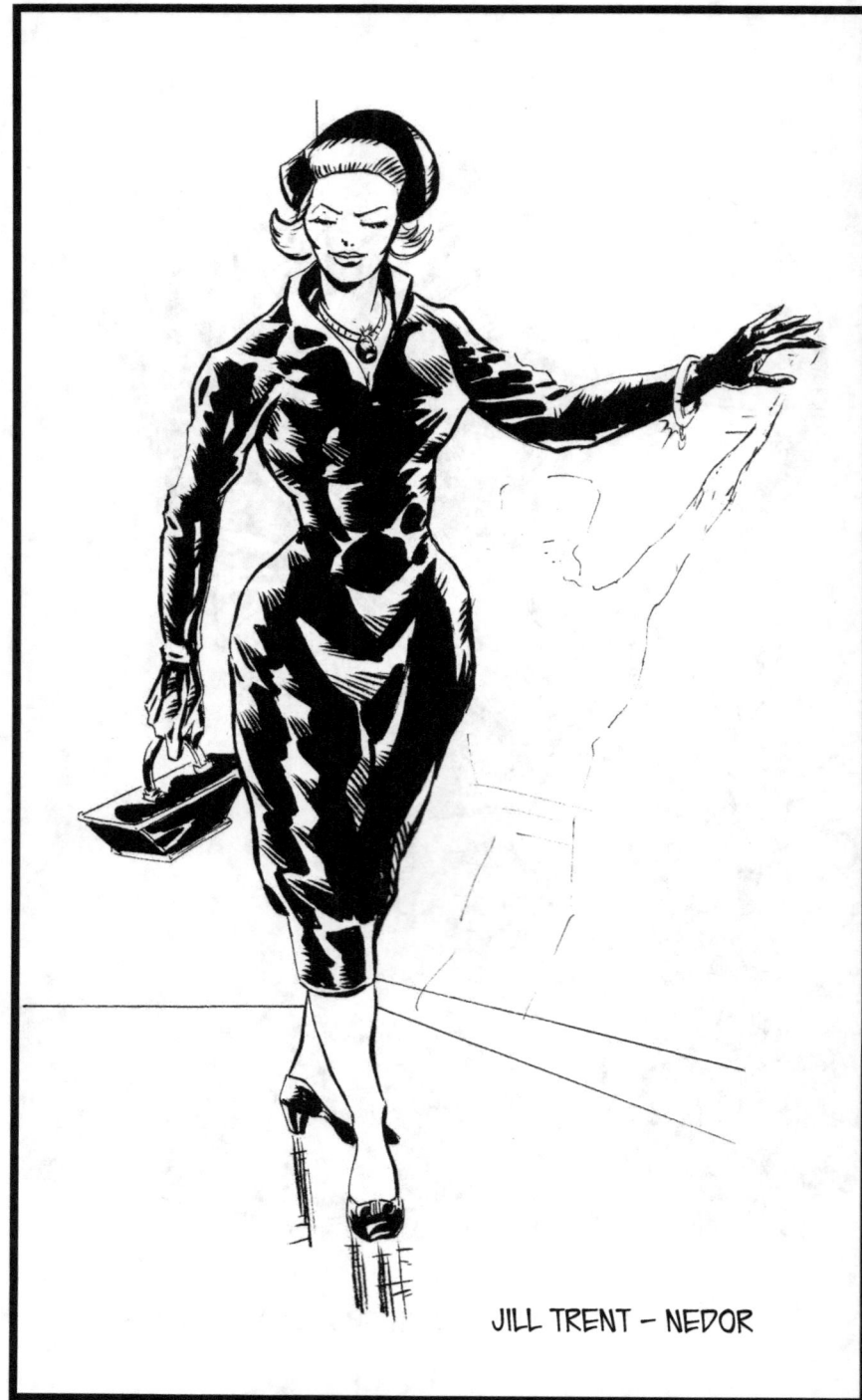

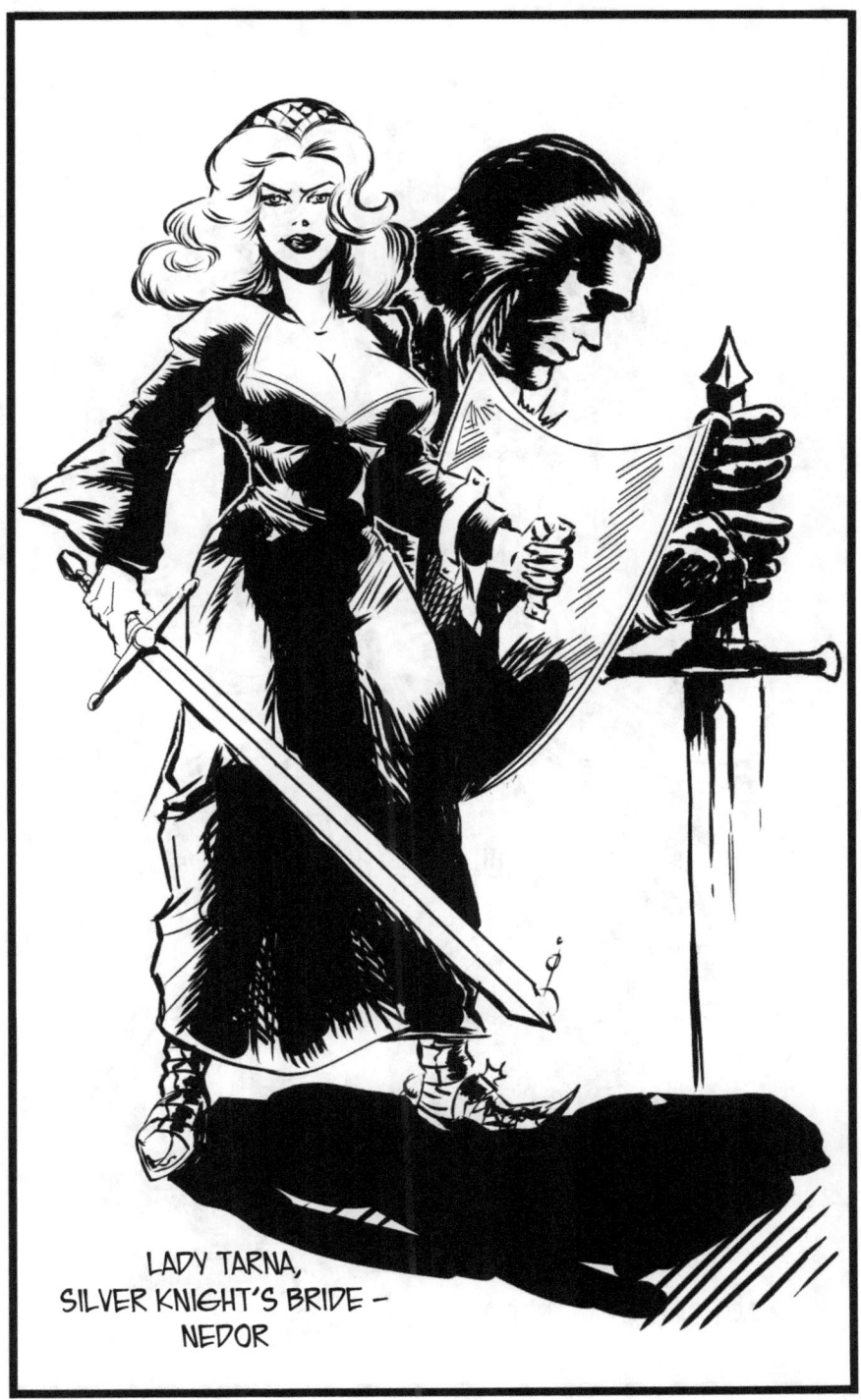

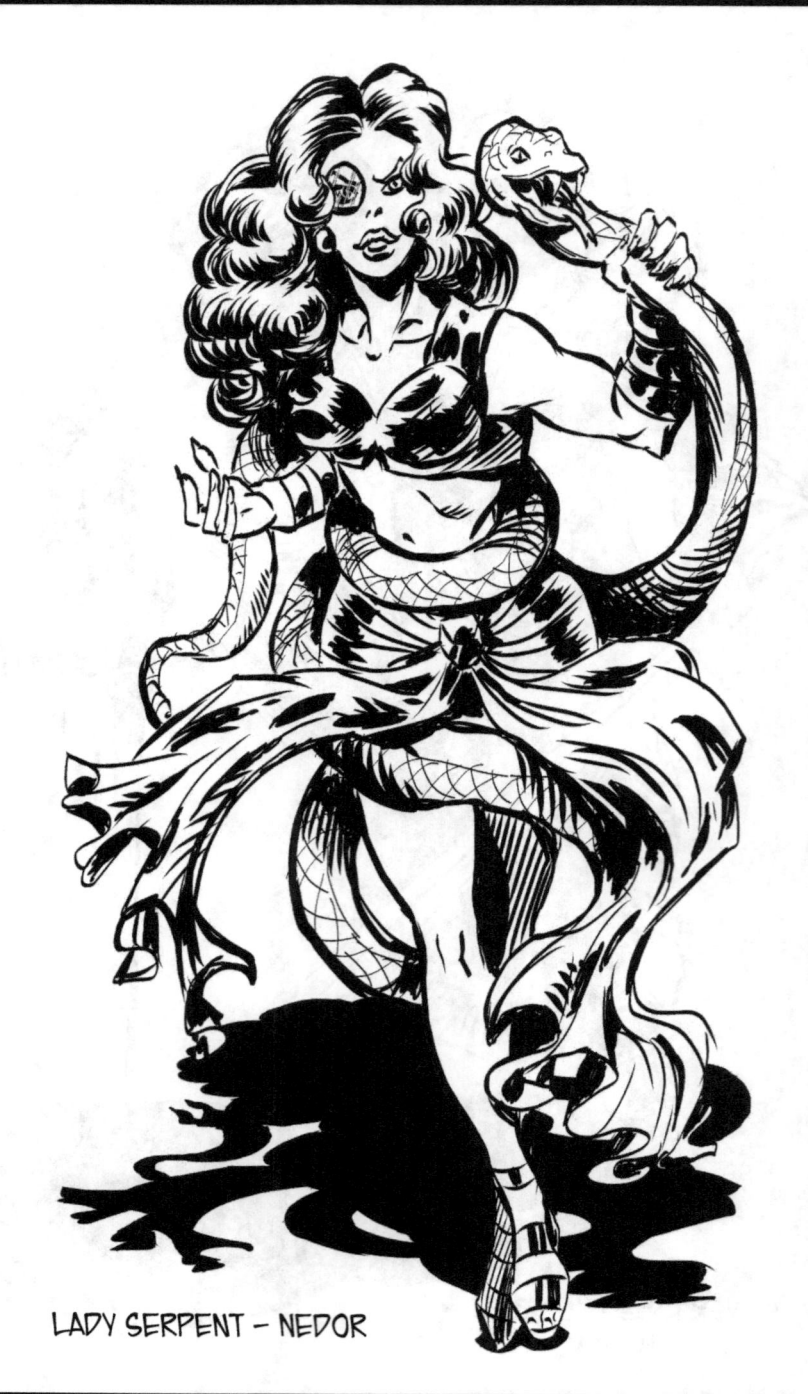

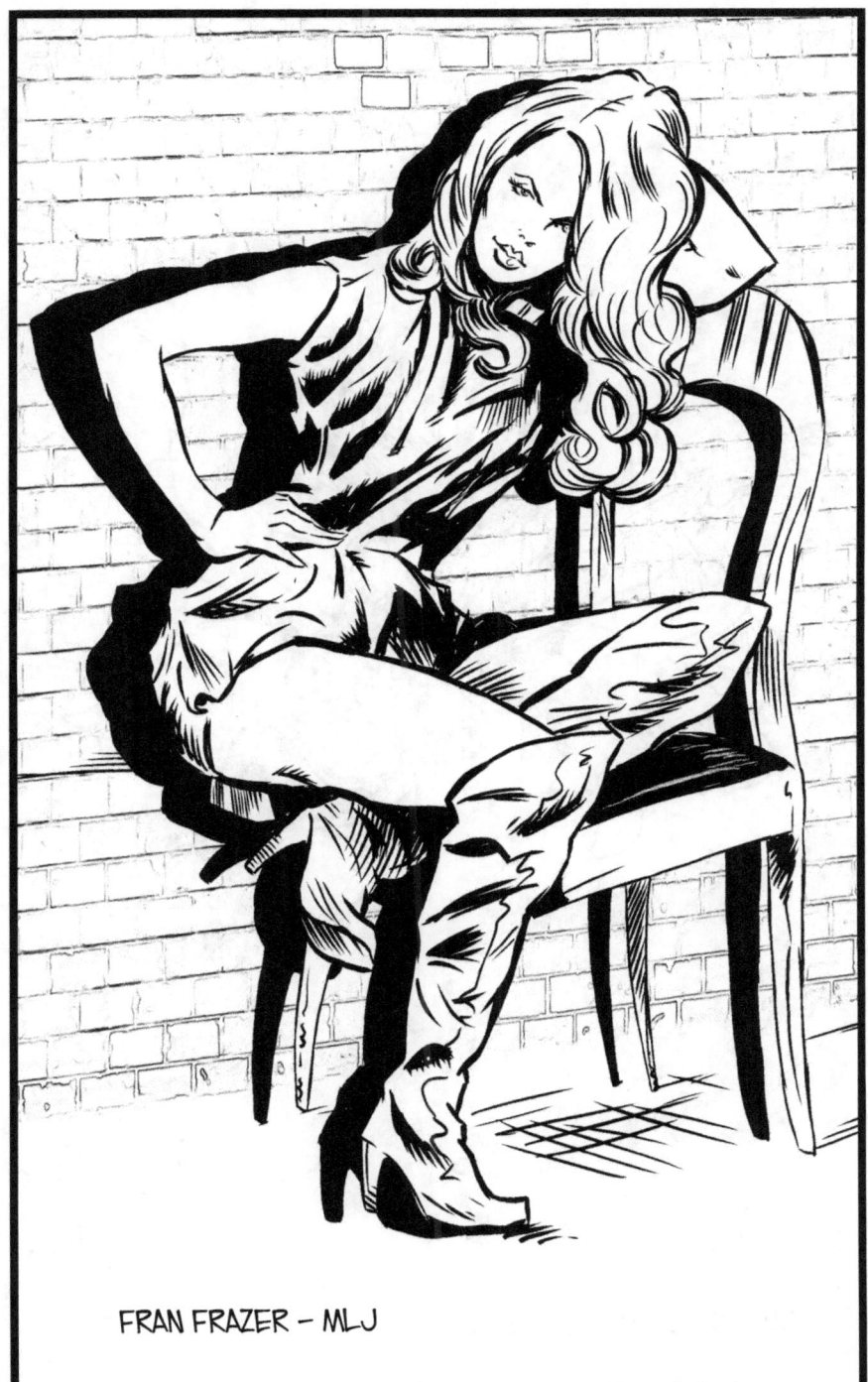

FRAN FRAZER - MLJ

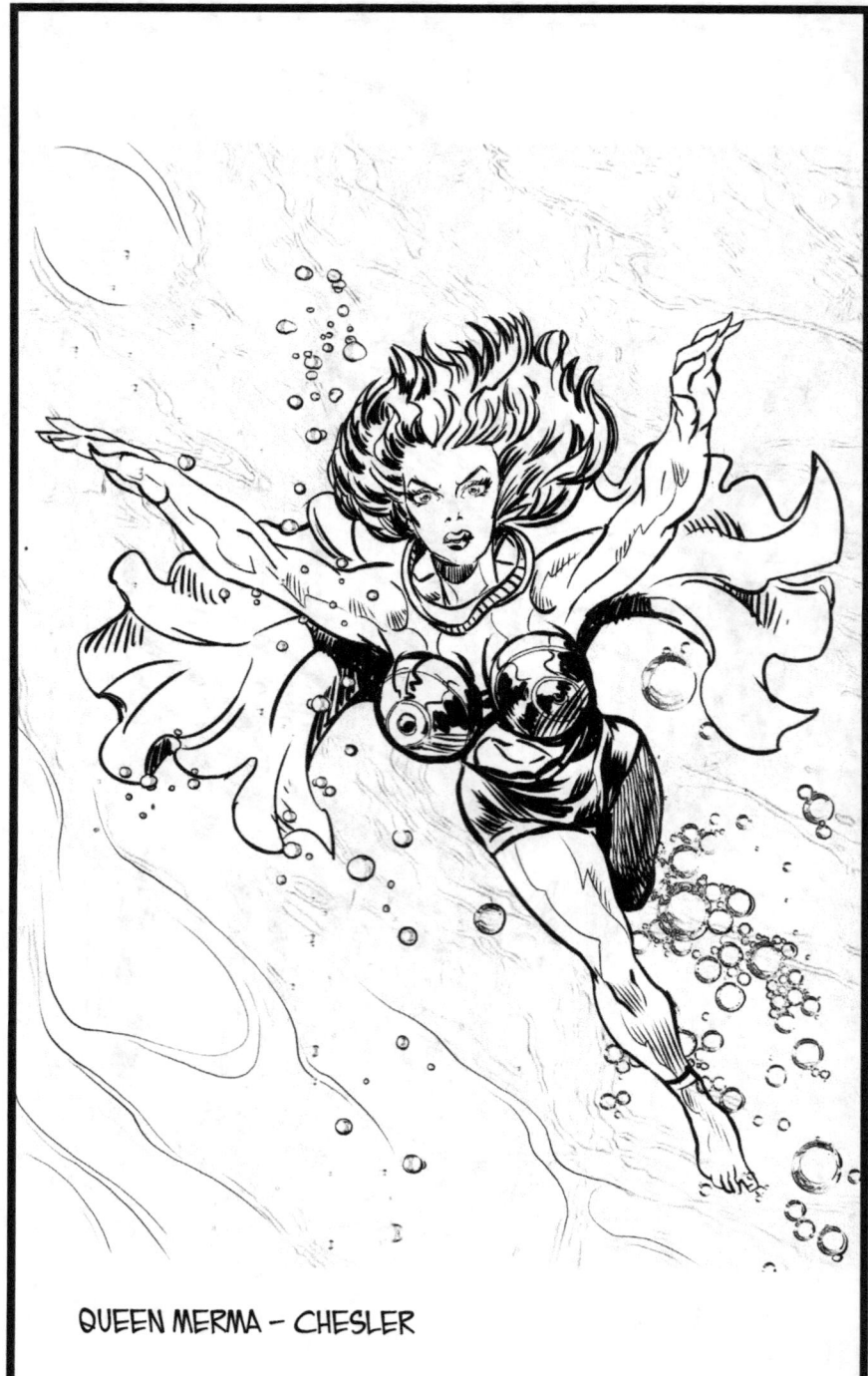

QUEEN MERMA – CHESLER

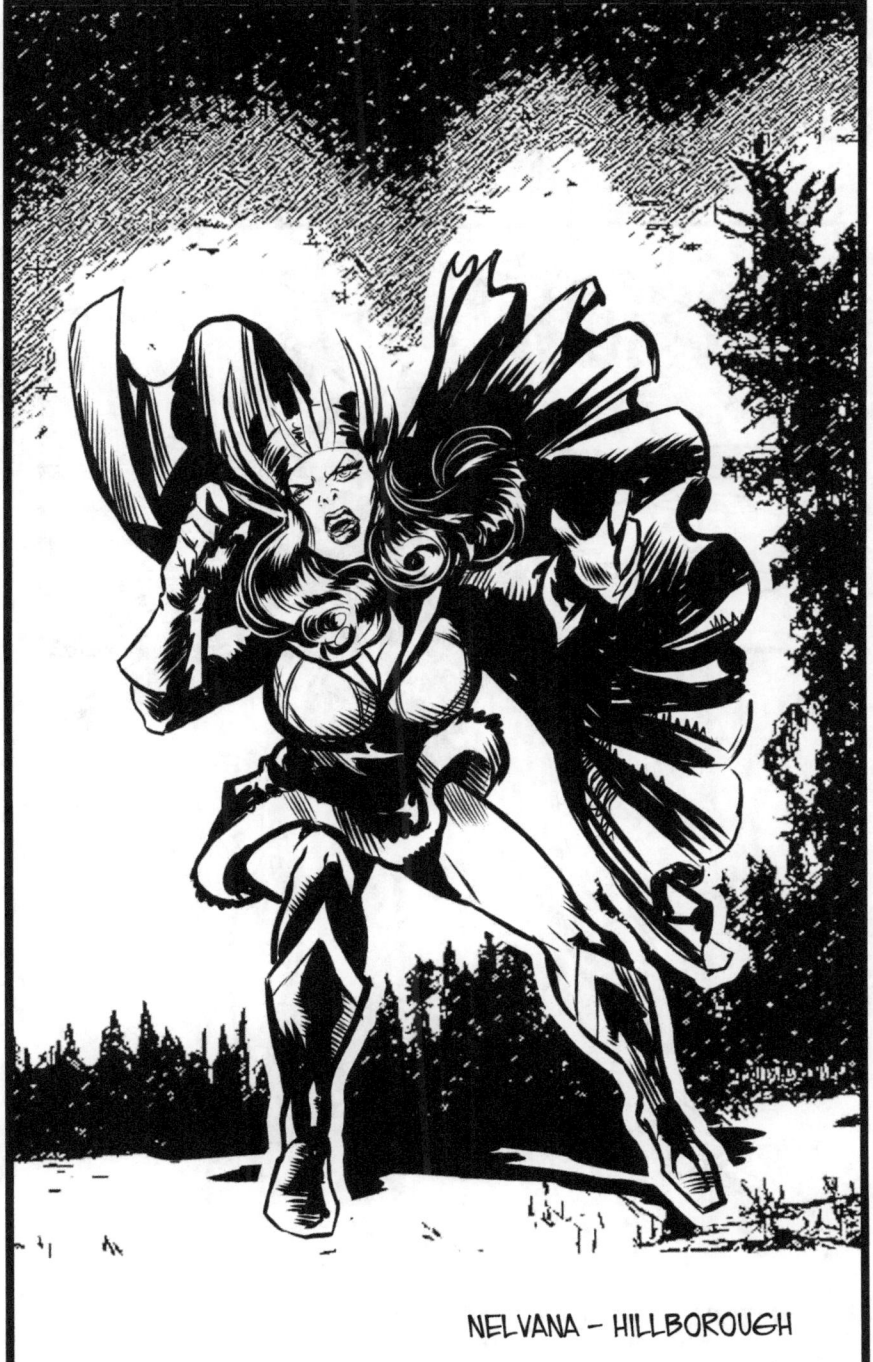

NELVANA - HILLBOROUGH

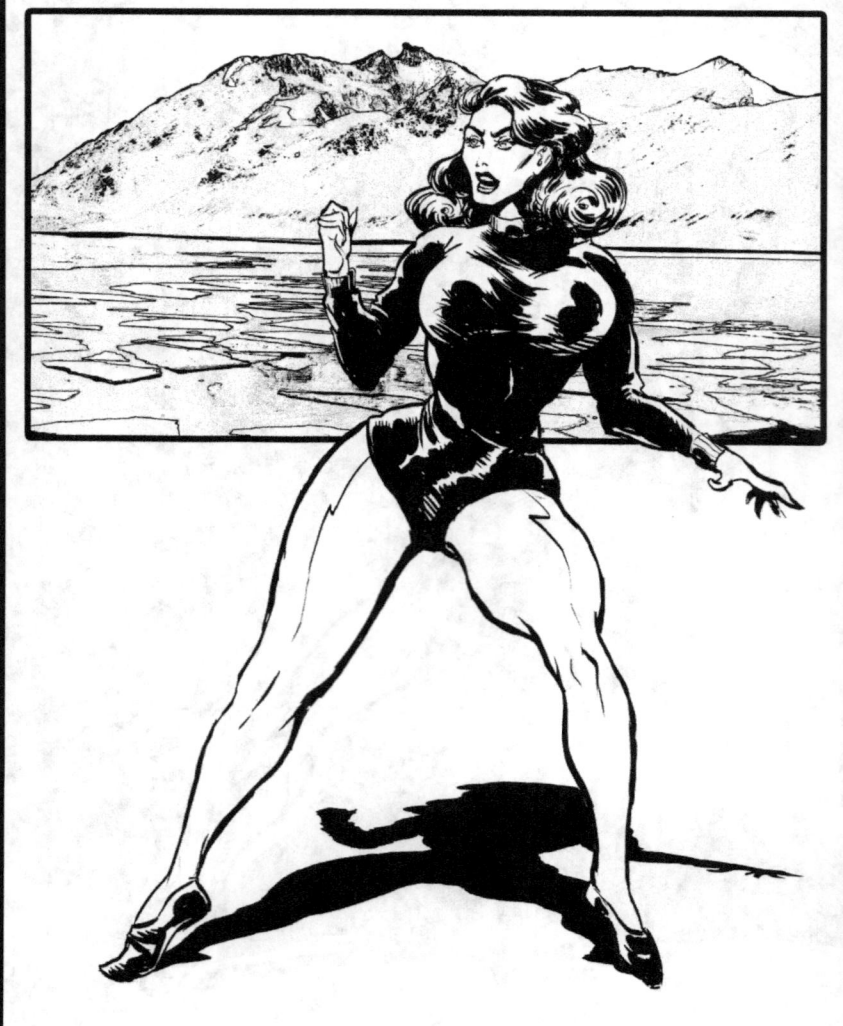

AMAZONA - FICTION HOUSE

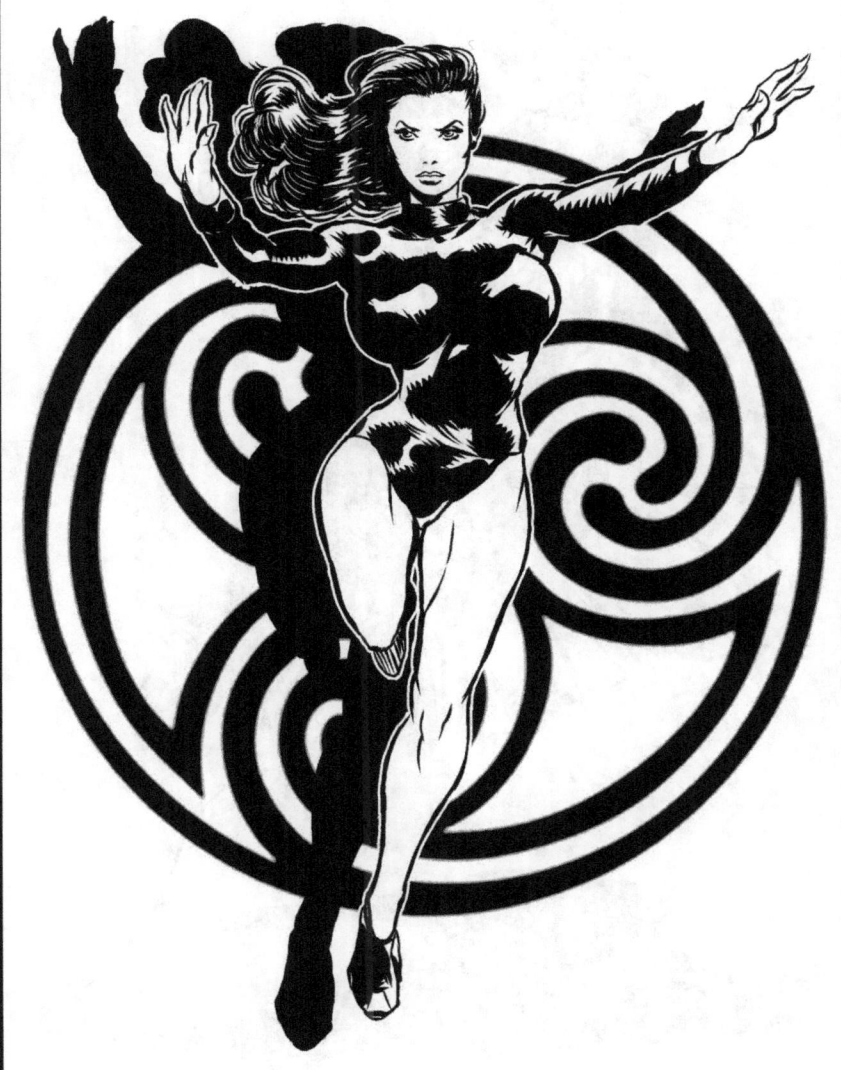

AMAZONA – FICTION HOUSE

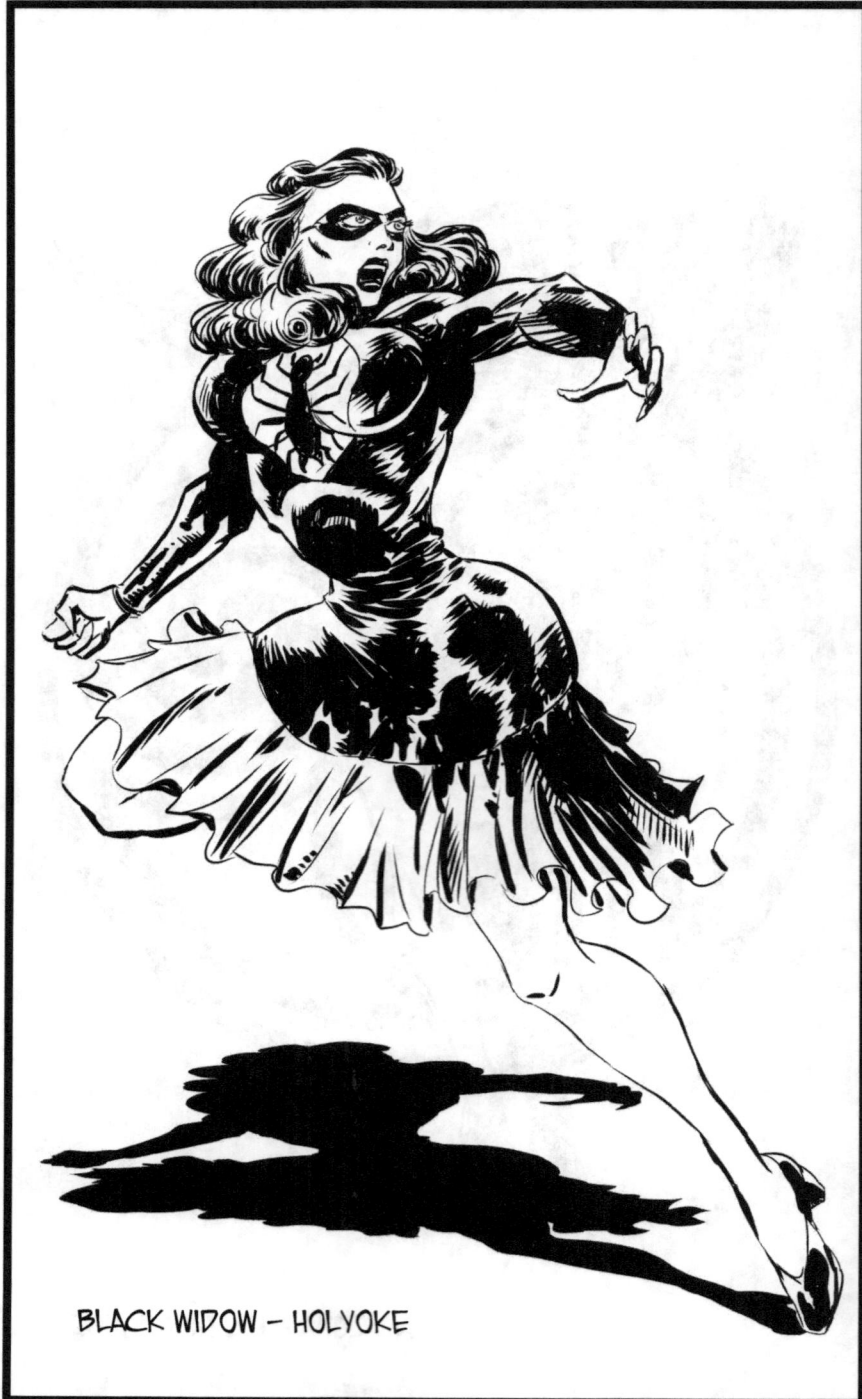

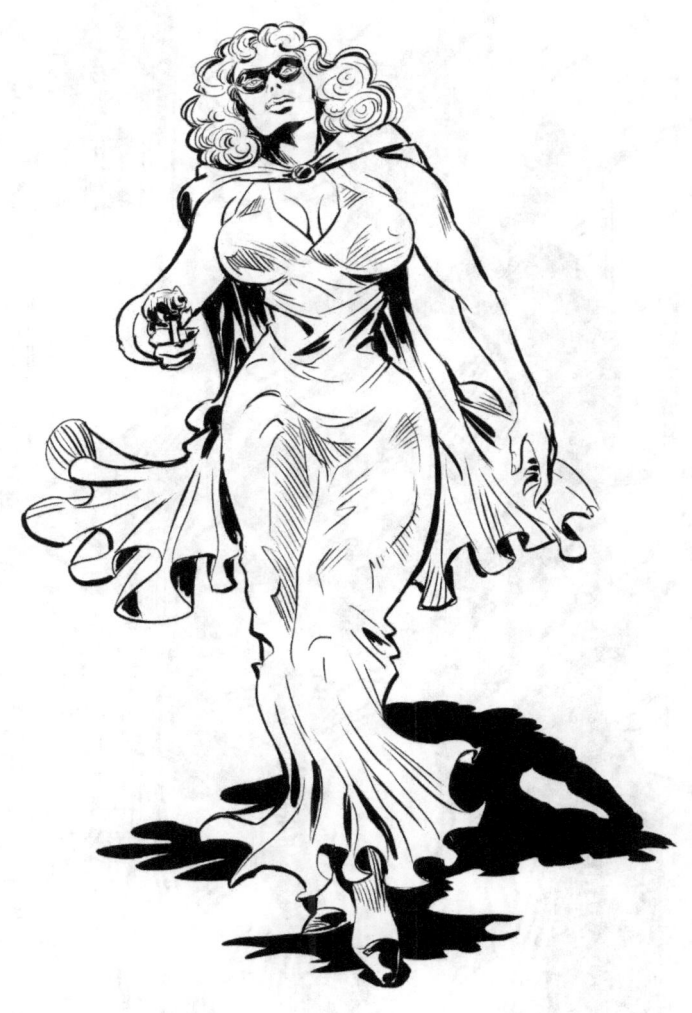

DOMINO LADY – FICTION HOUSE

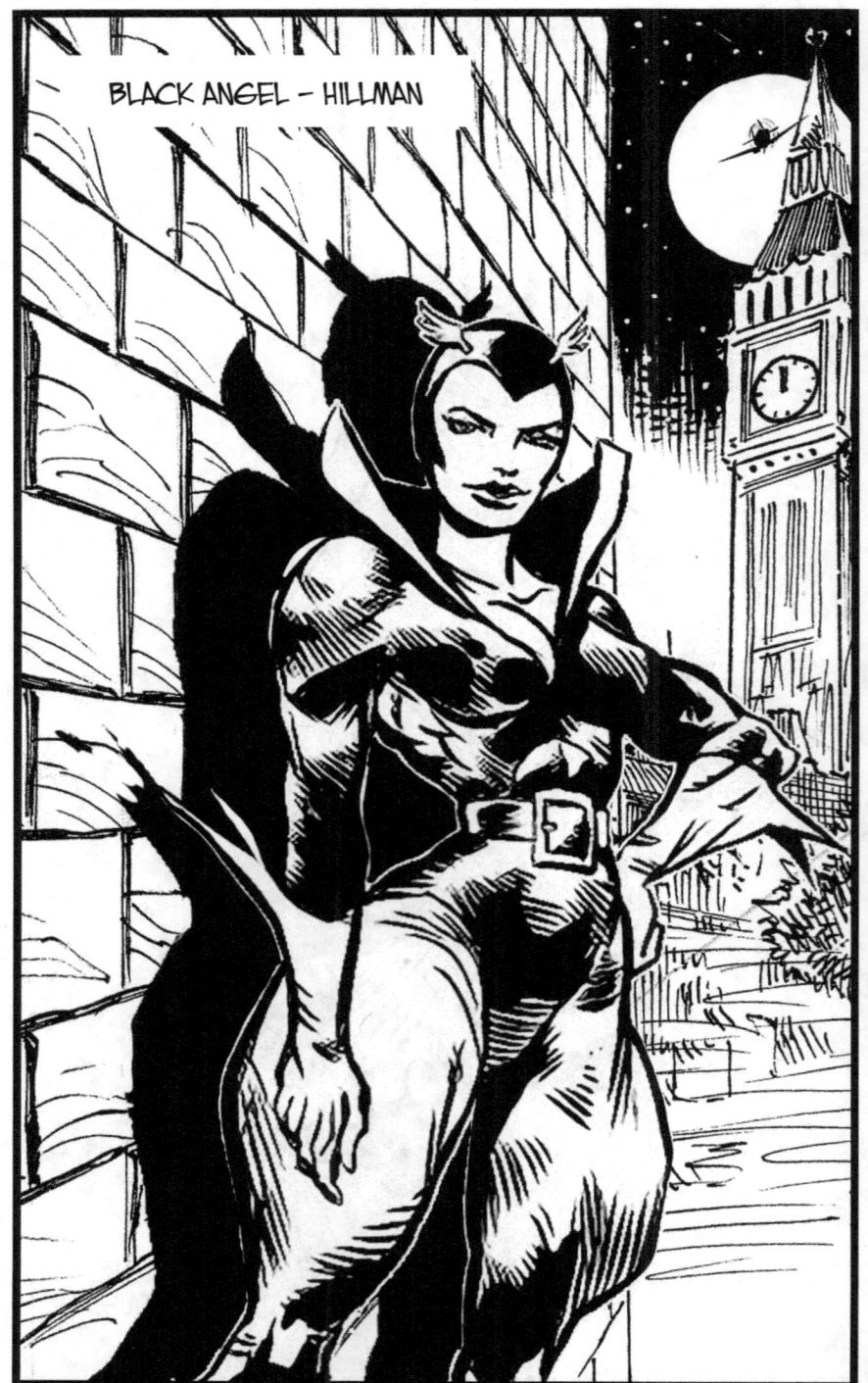

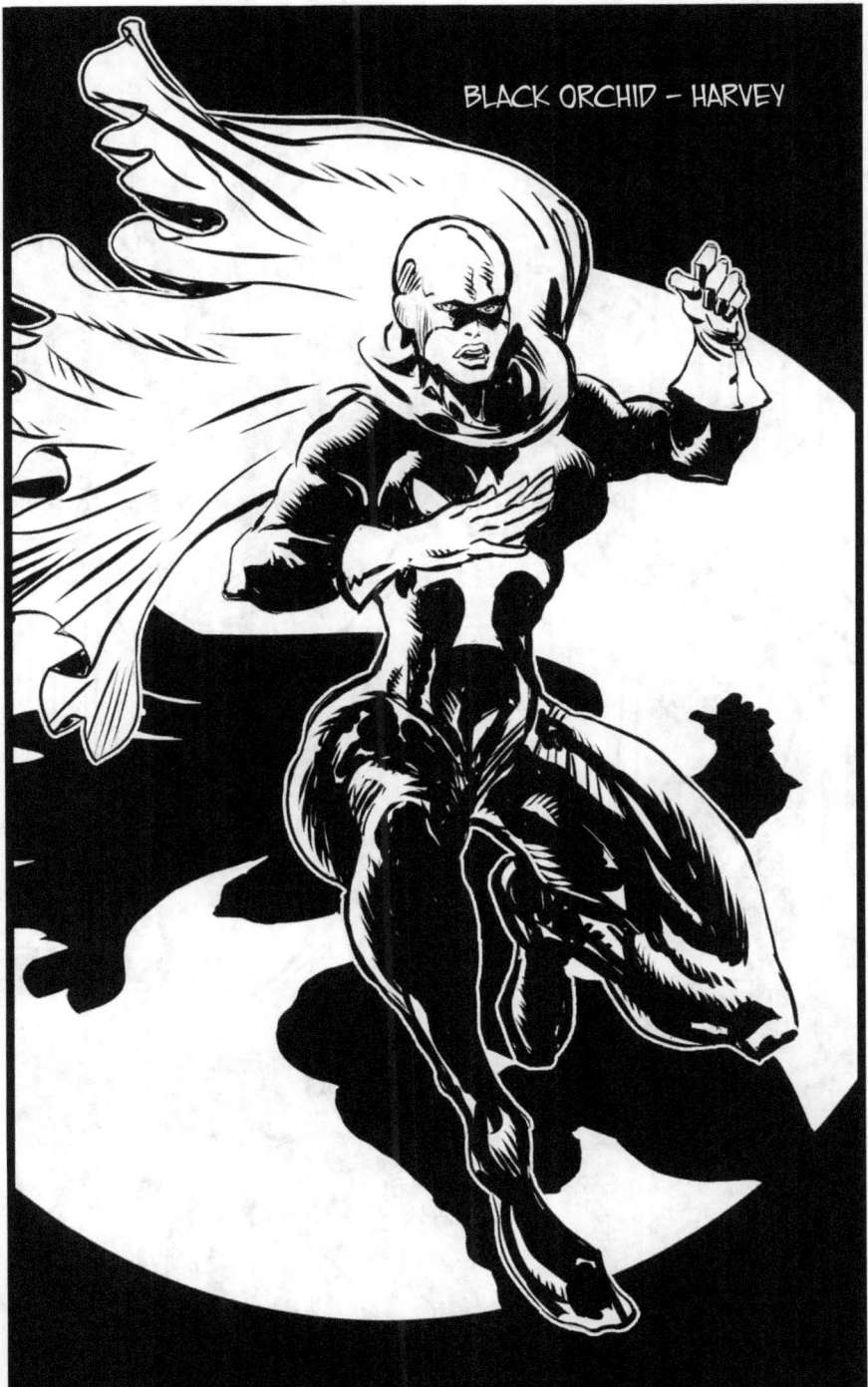

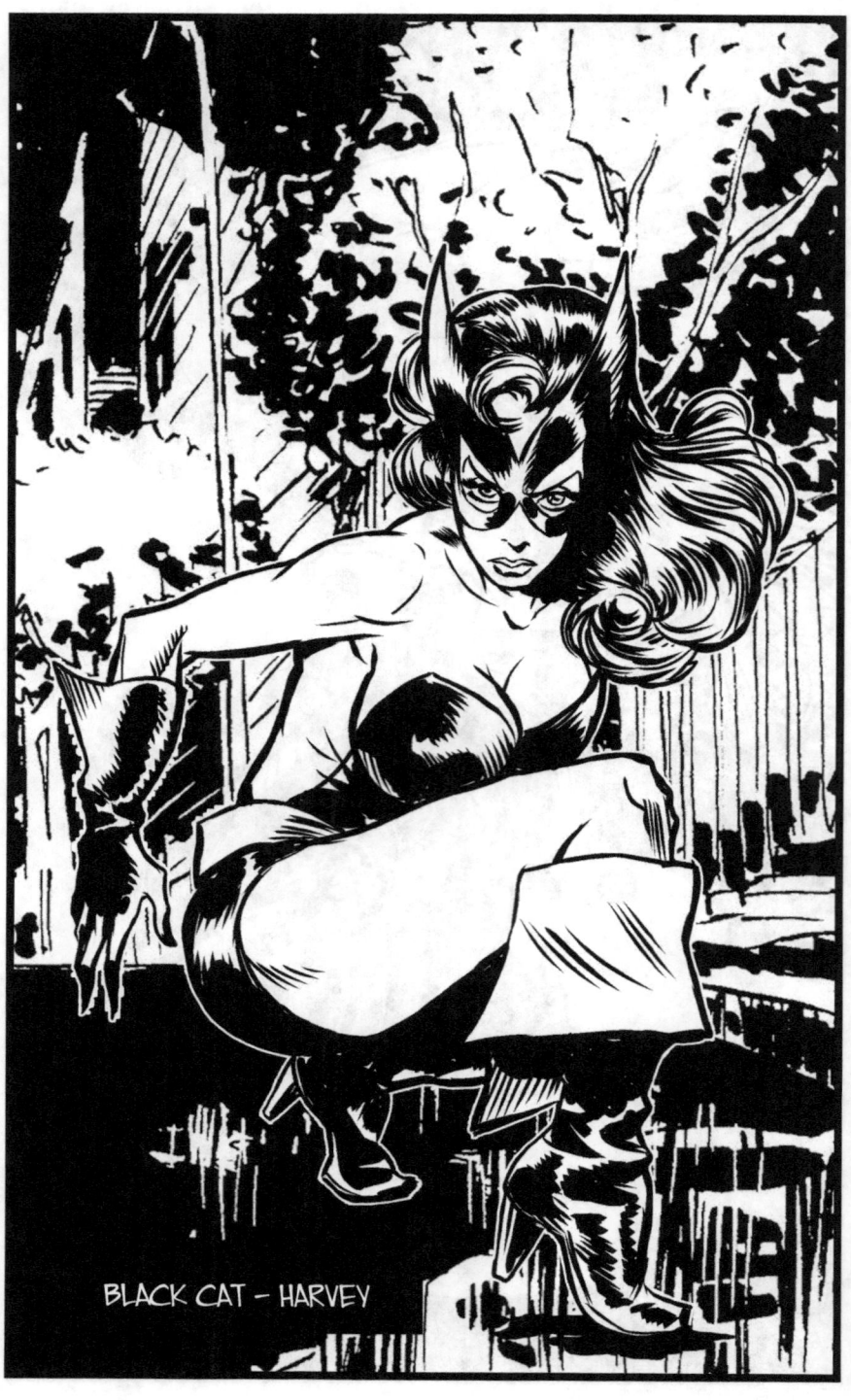

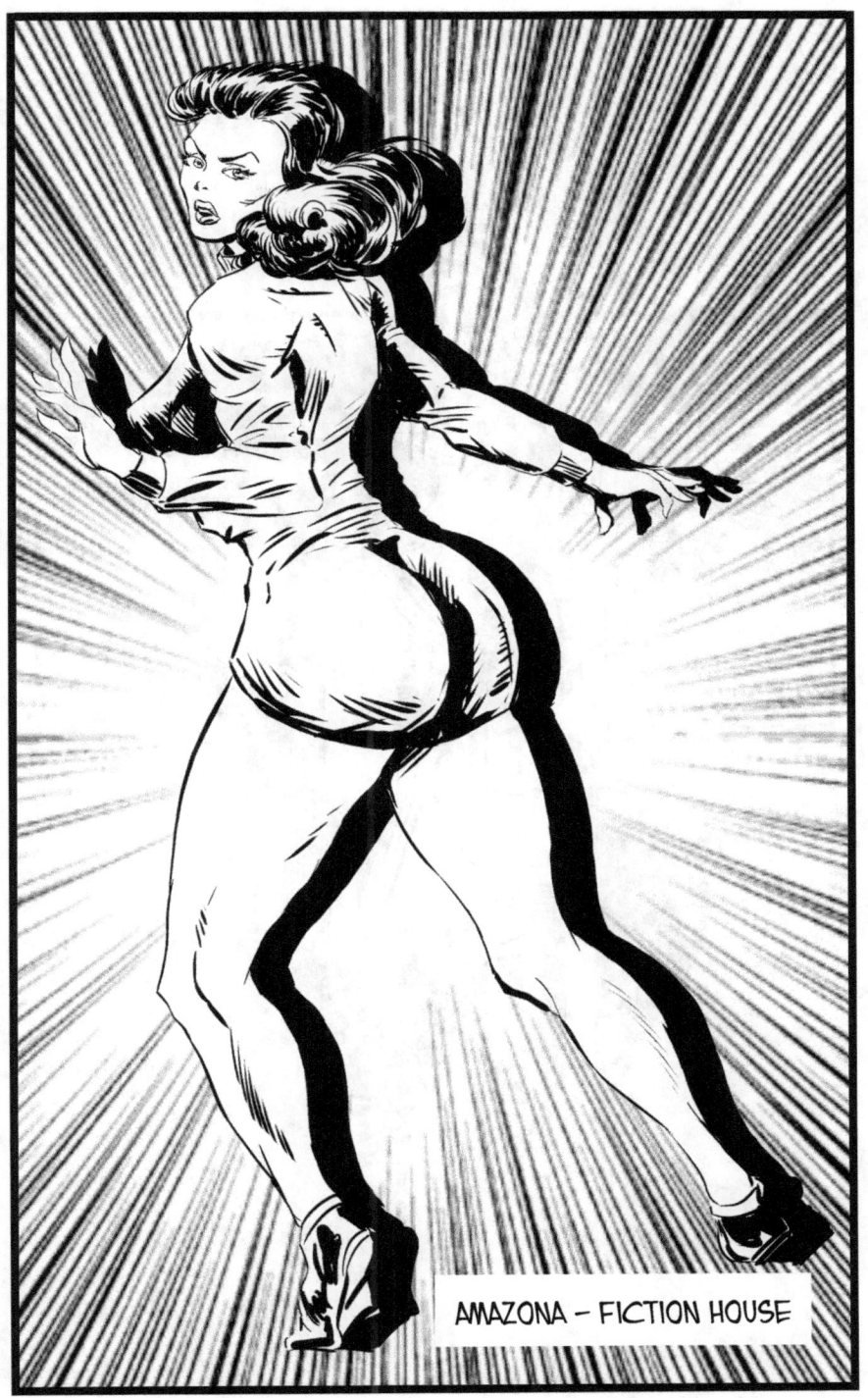

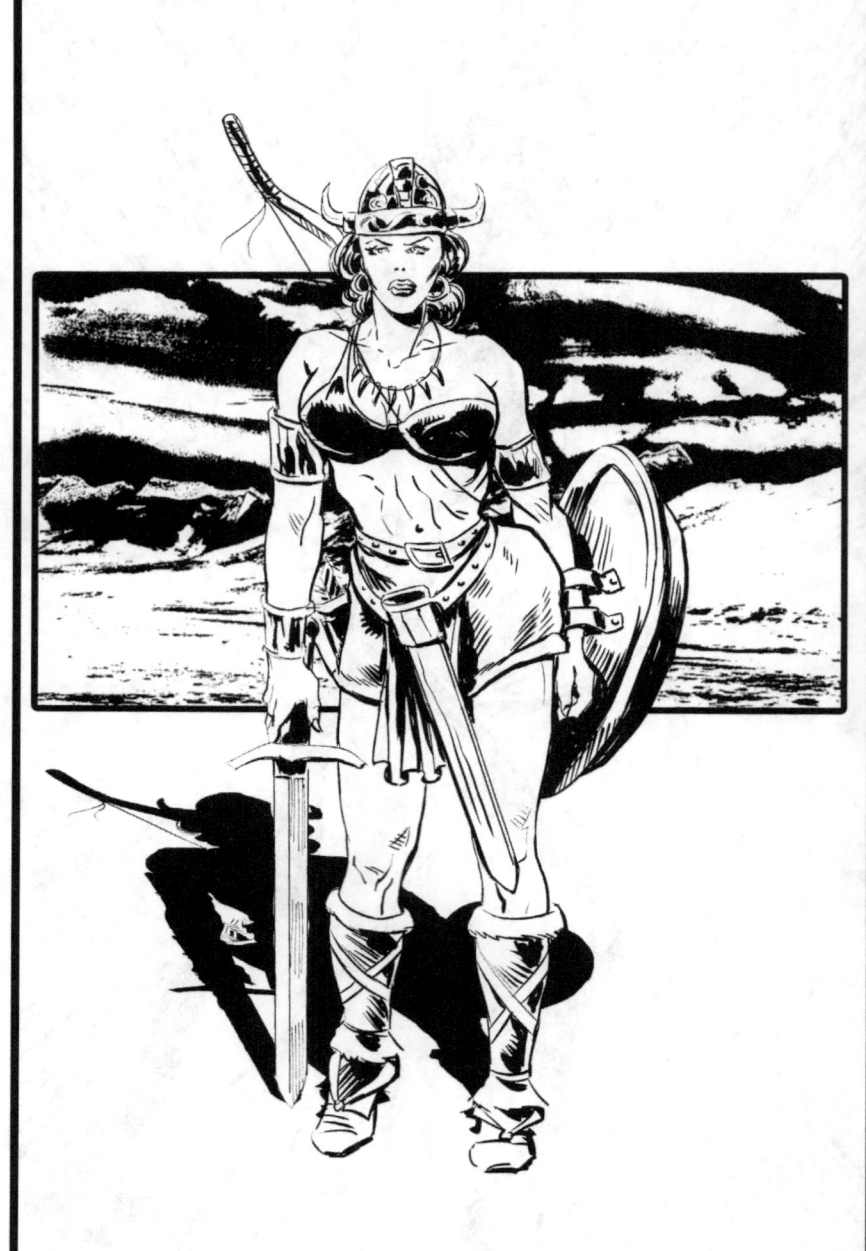

DARA OF THE VIKINGS - AVON

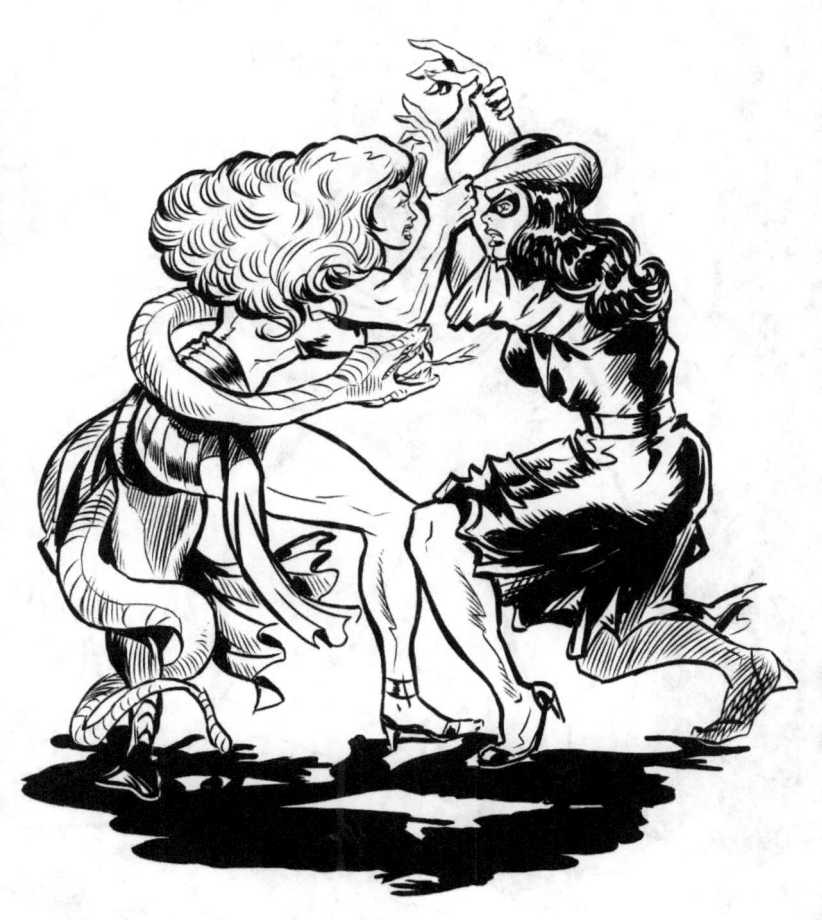

LADY SERPENT VS RED ANN - NEDOR

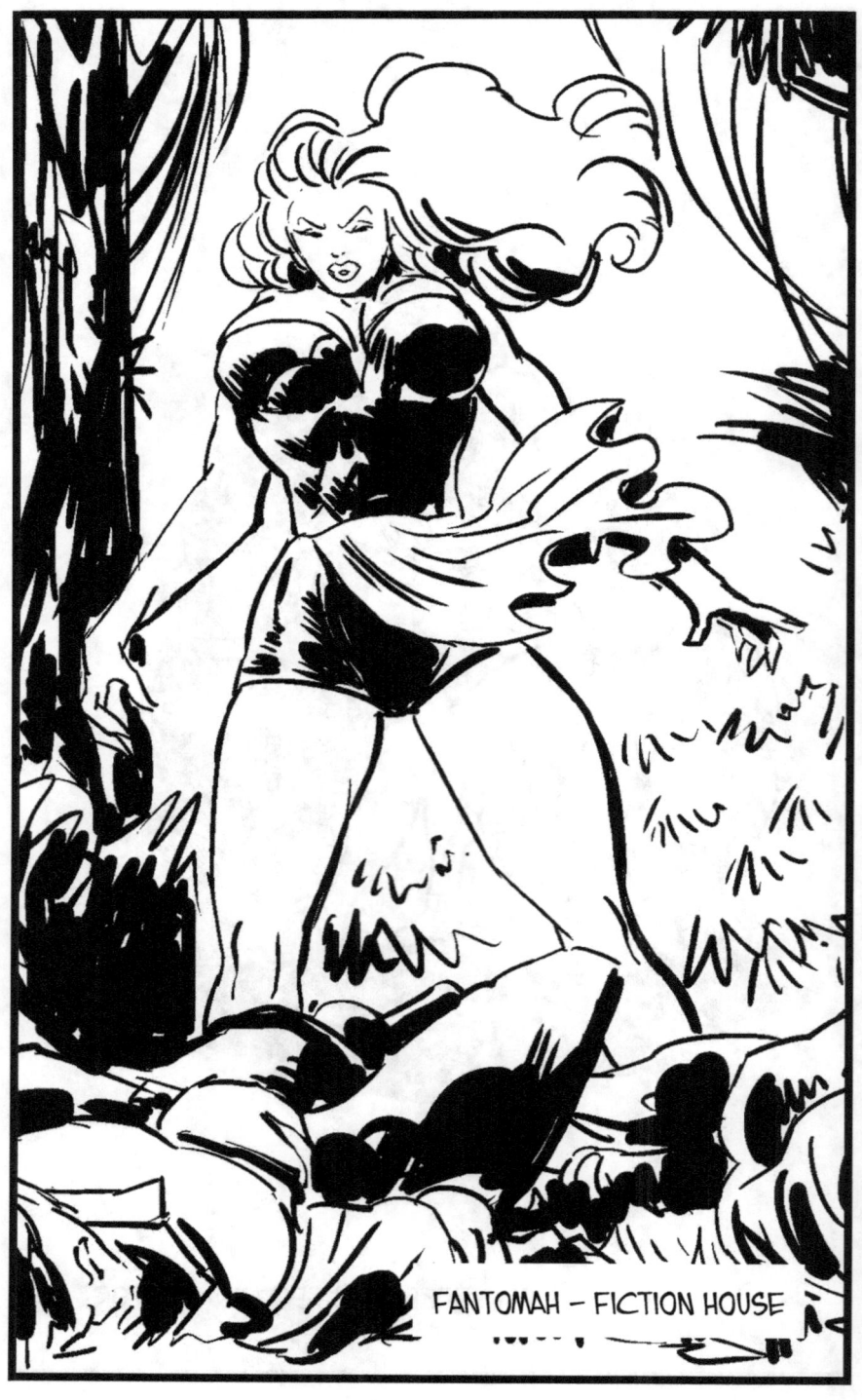

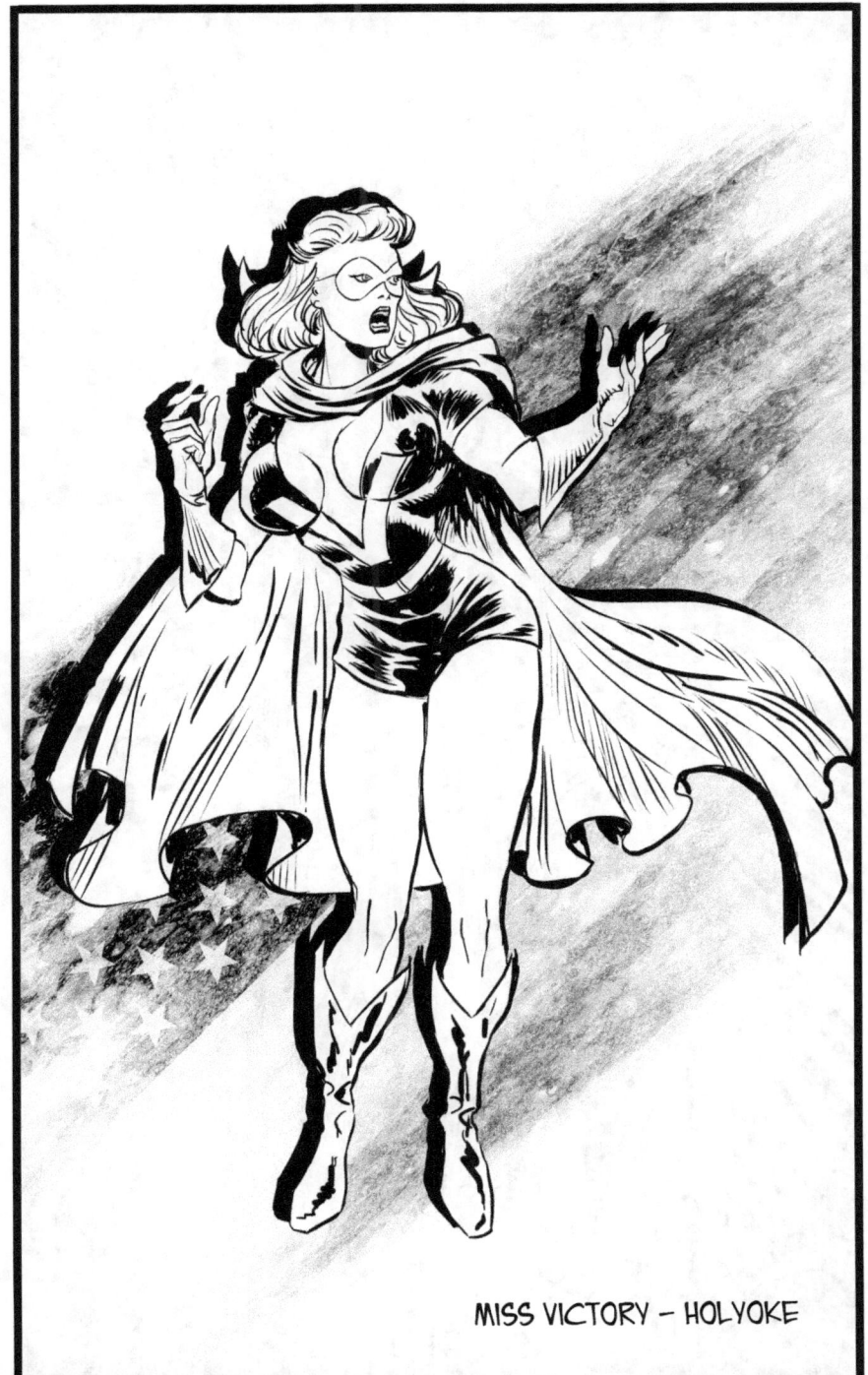

MISS VICTORY - HOLYOKE

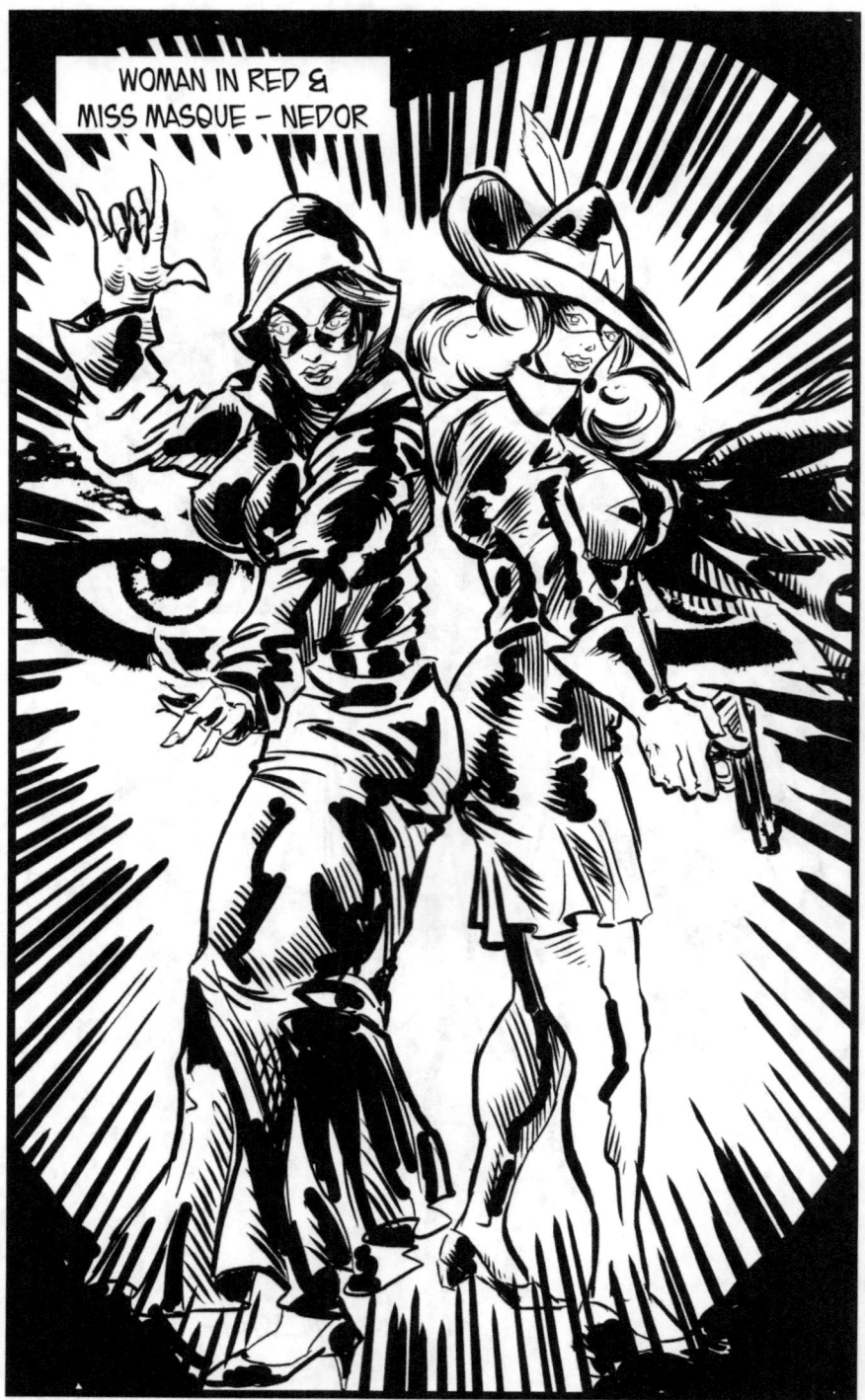

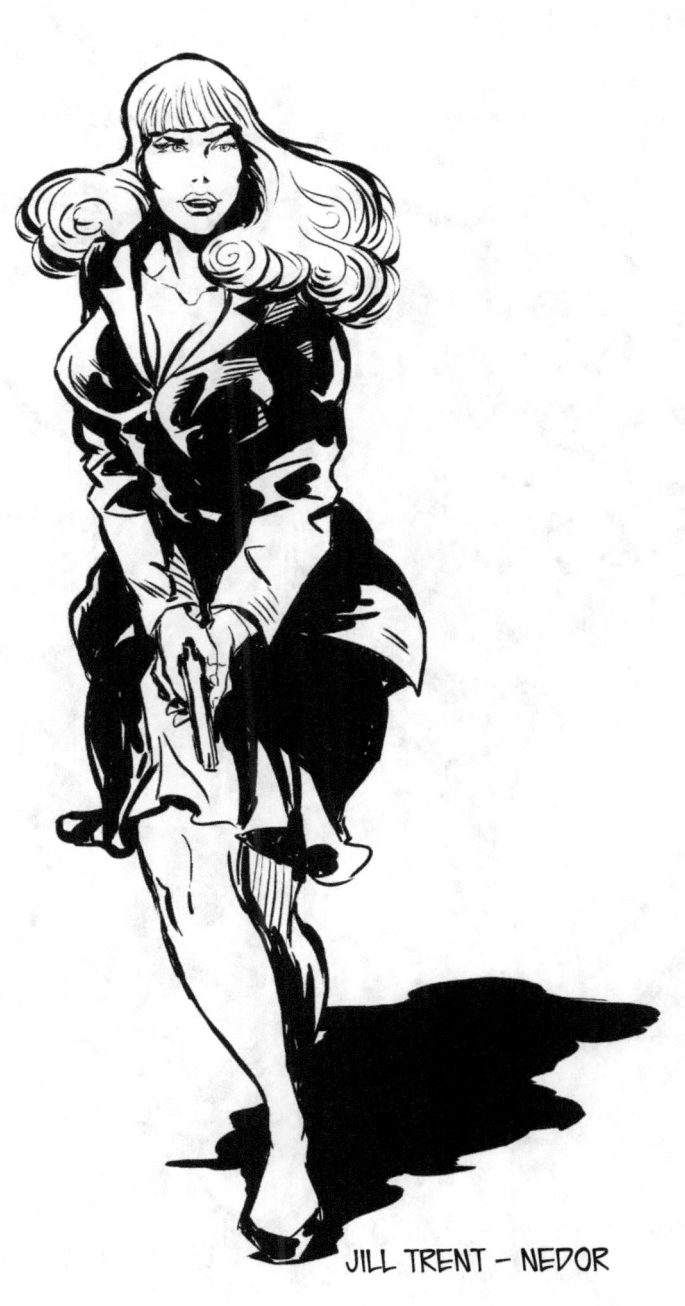

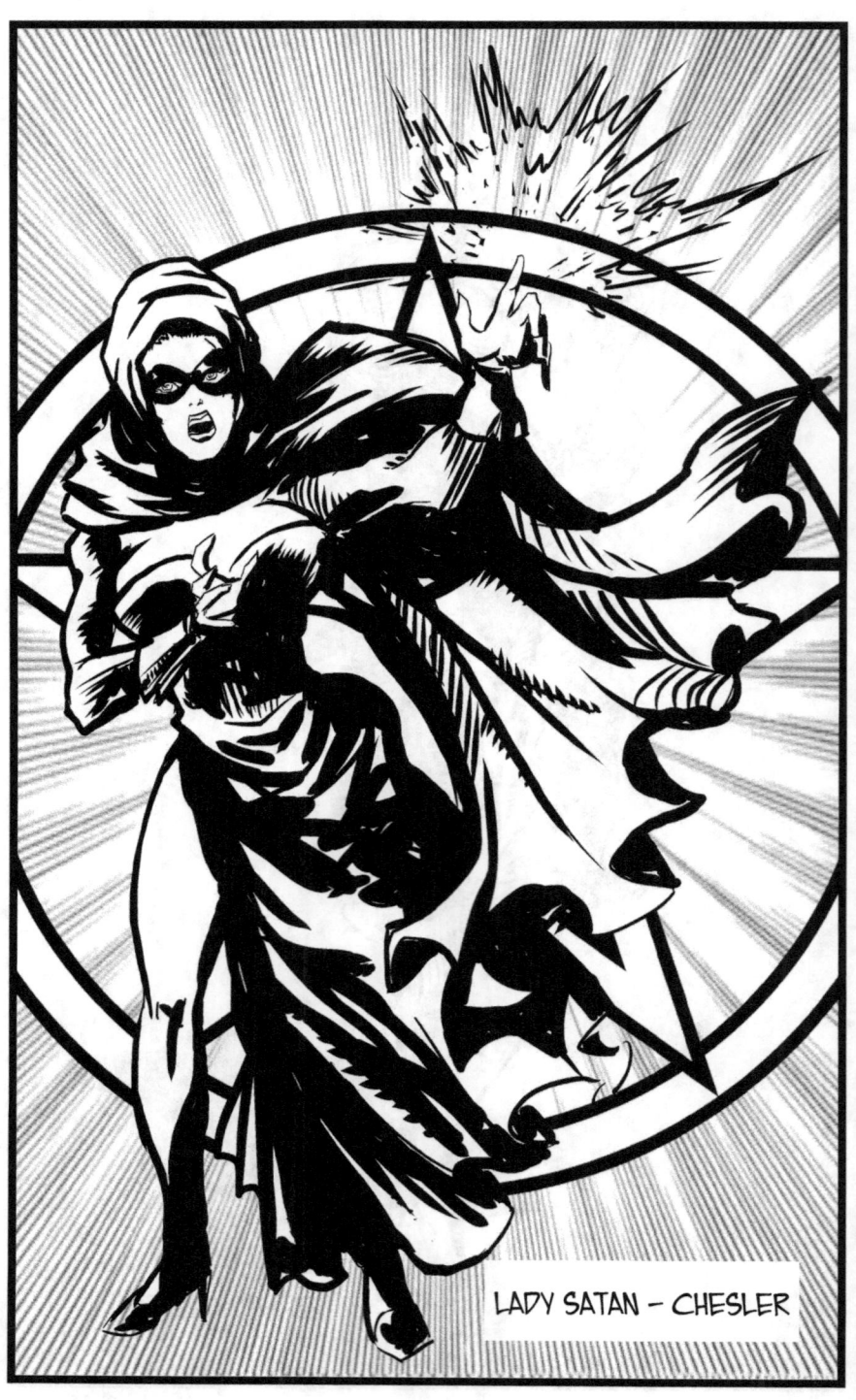

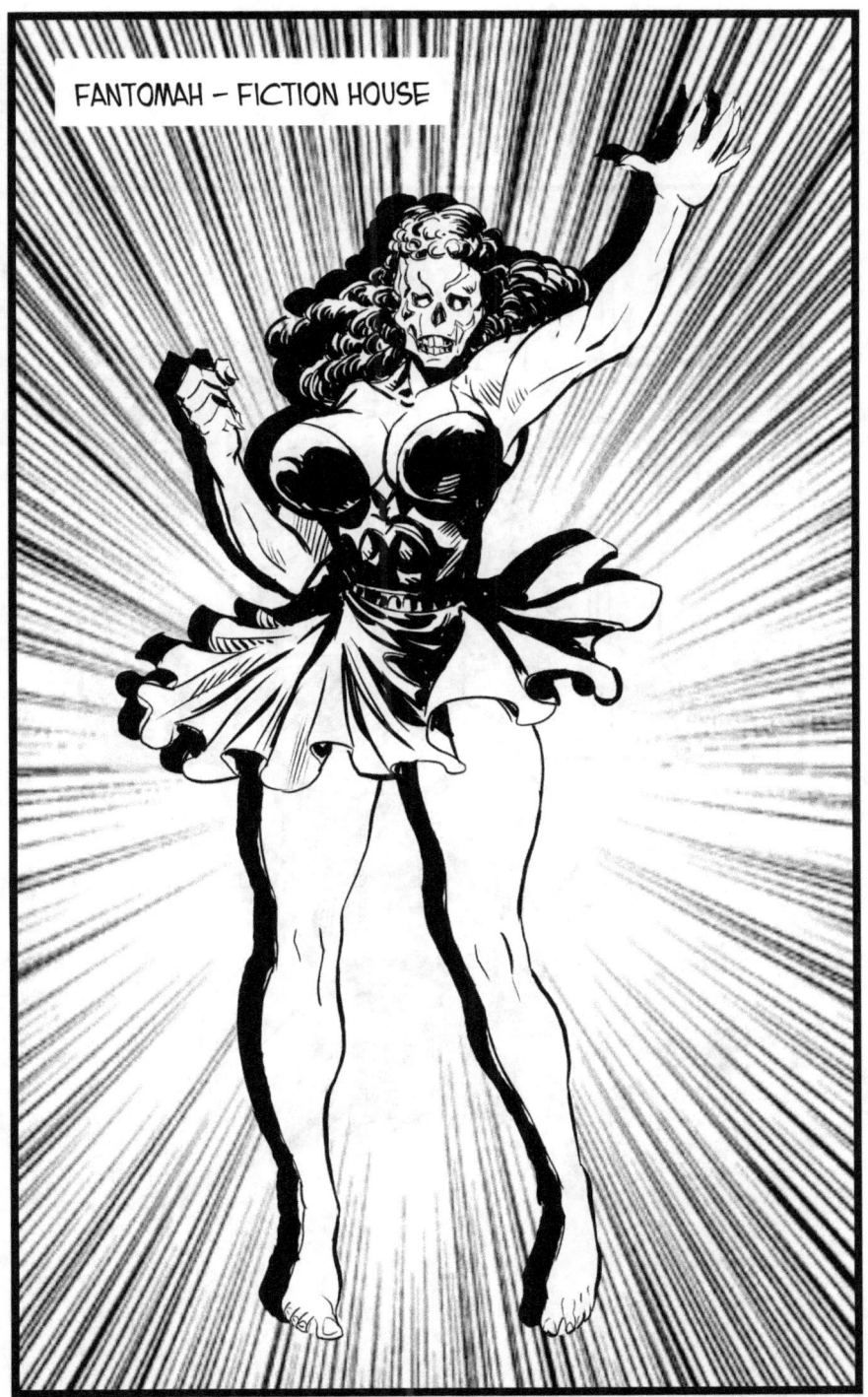

JILL TRENT - NEDOR

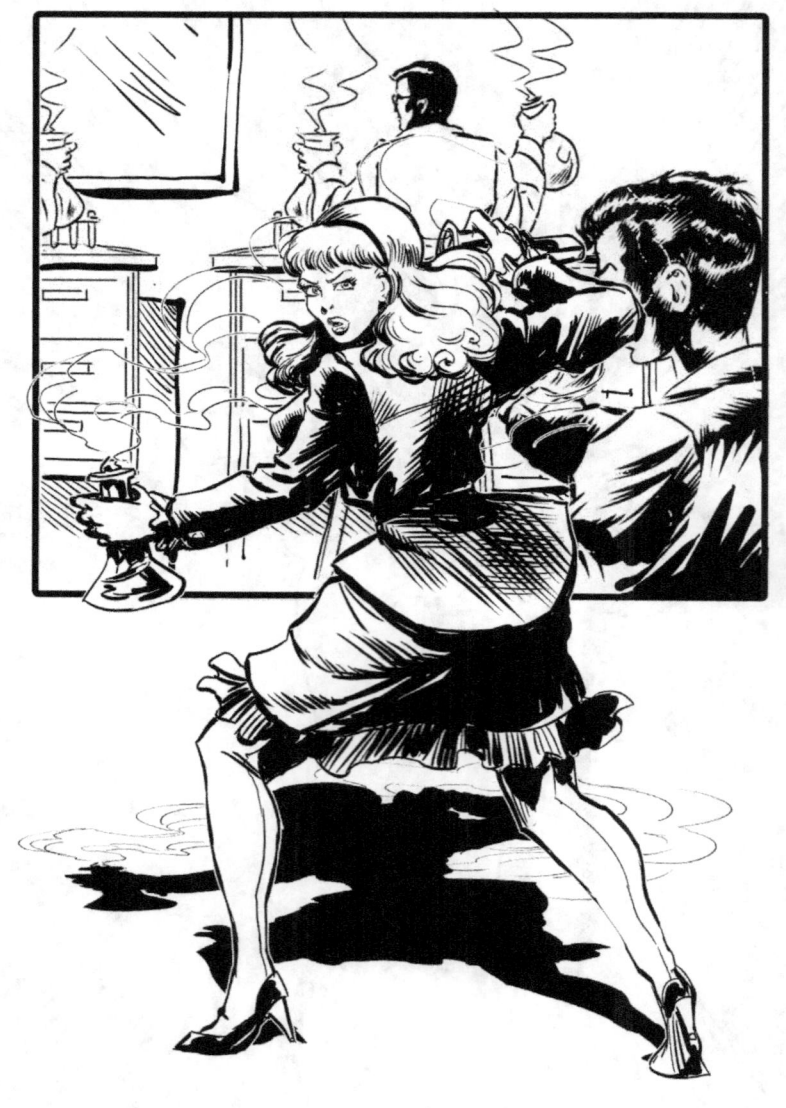

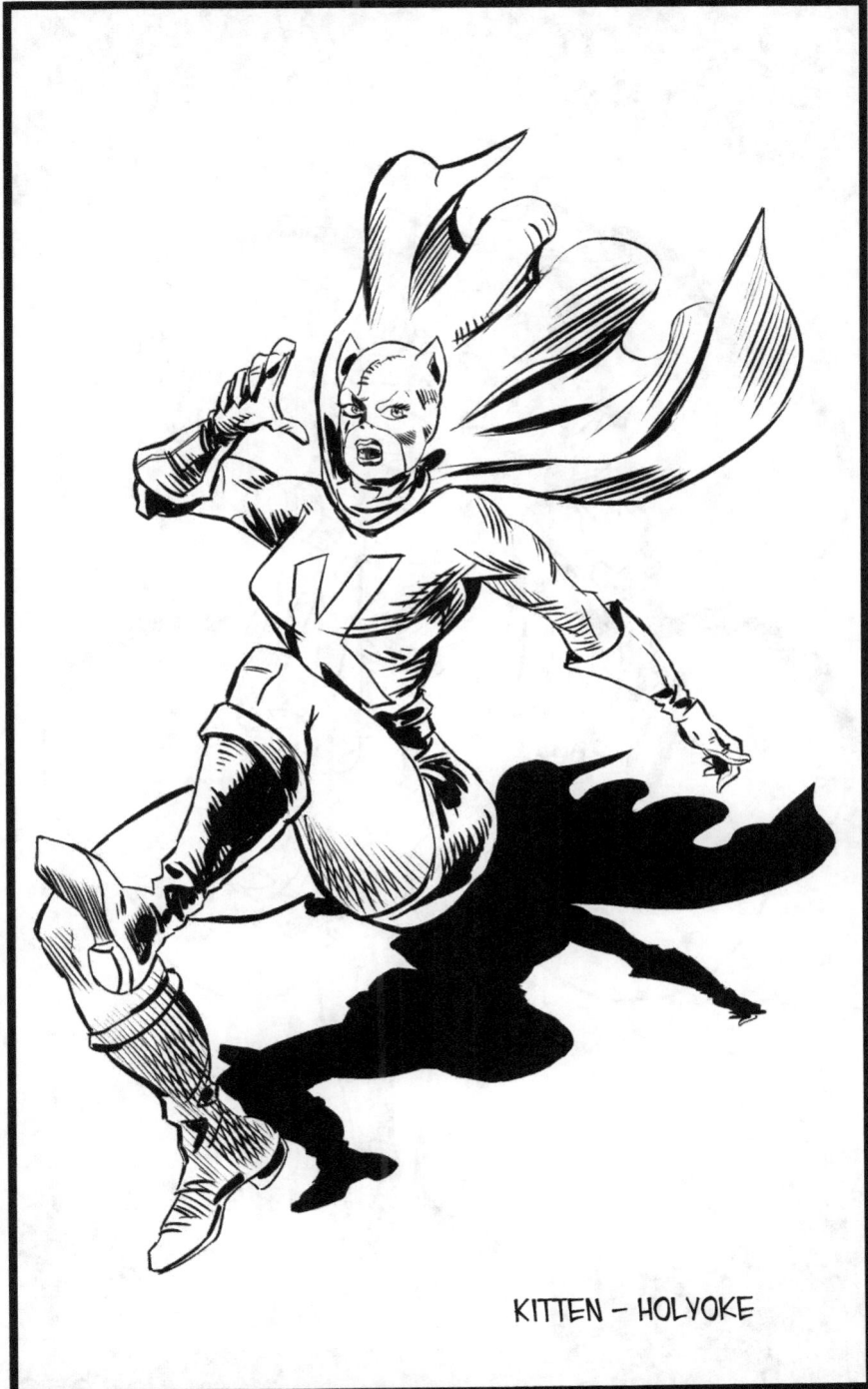
KITTEN - HOLYOKE

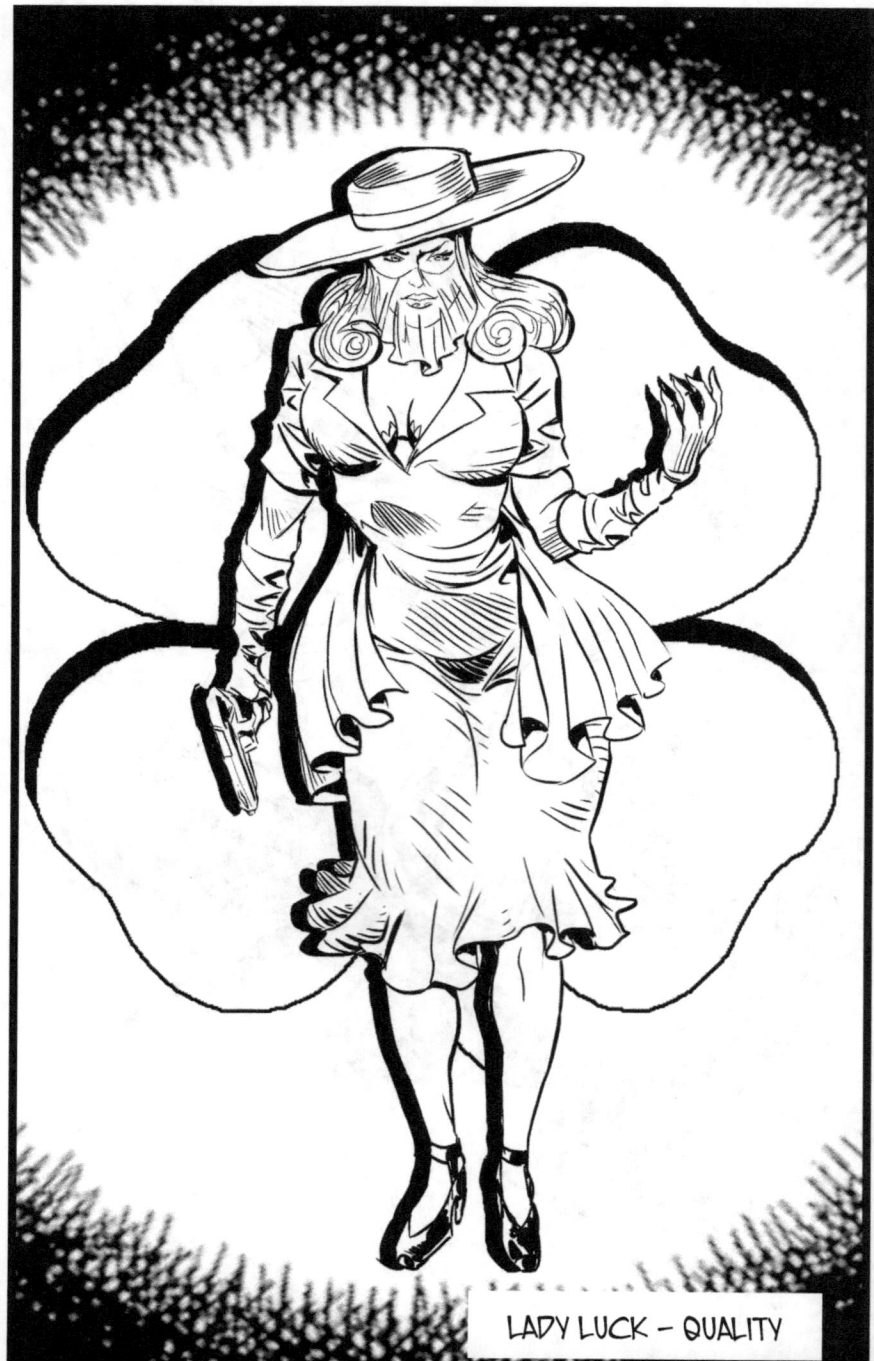

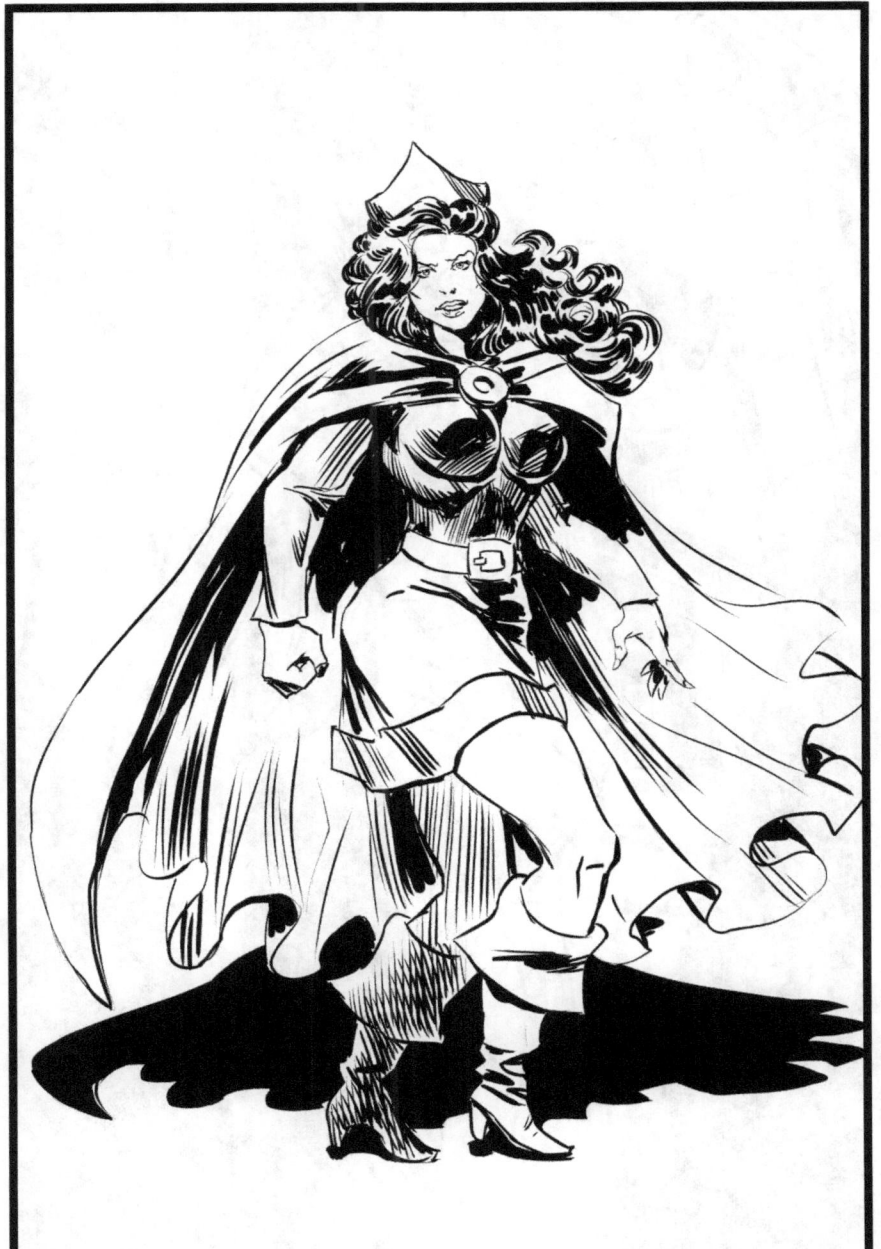

LADY FAIRPLAY - PROGRESSIVE

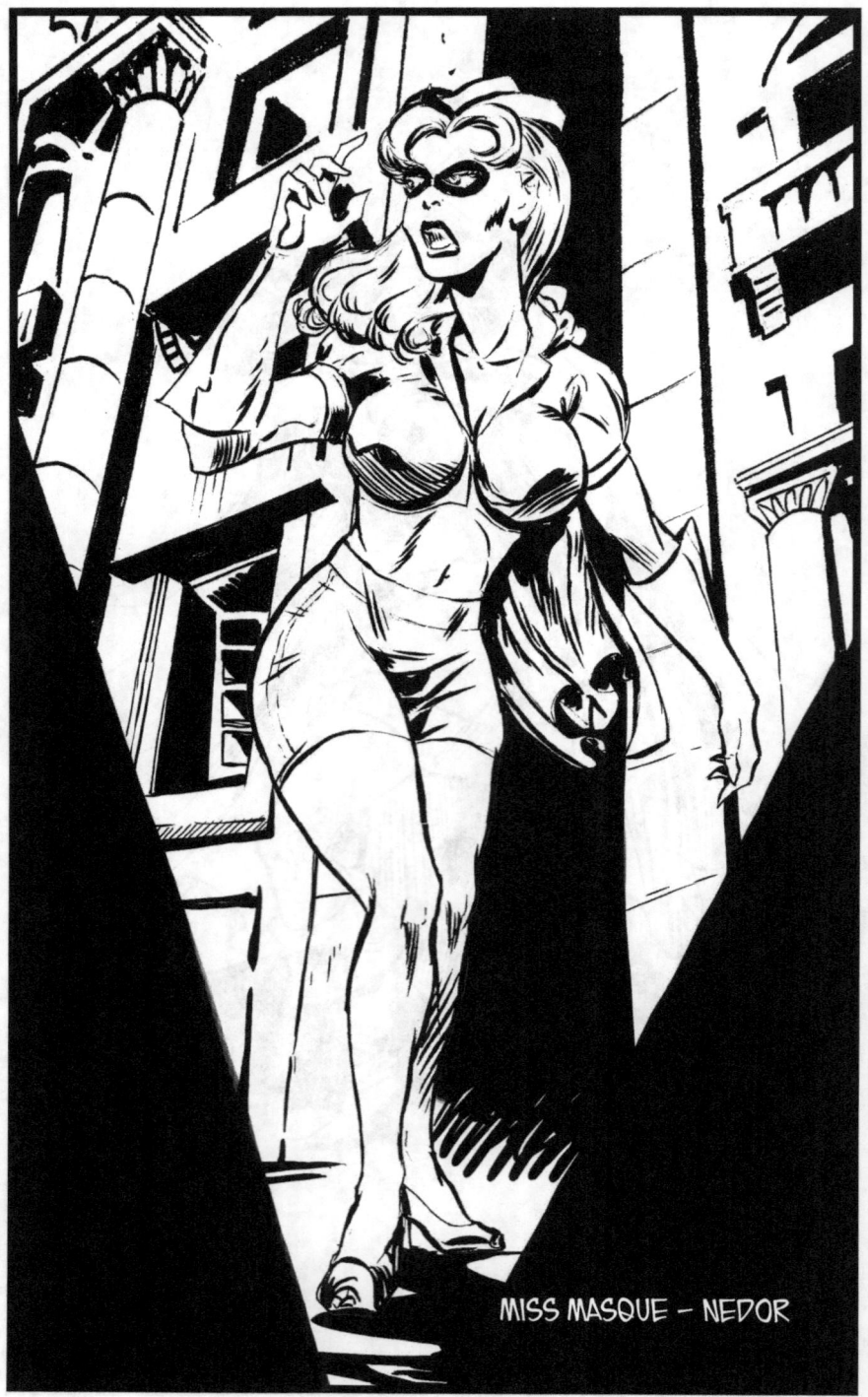

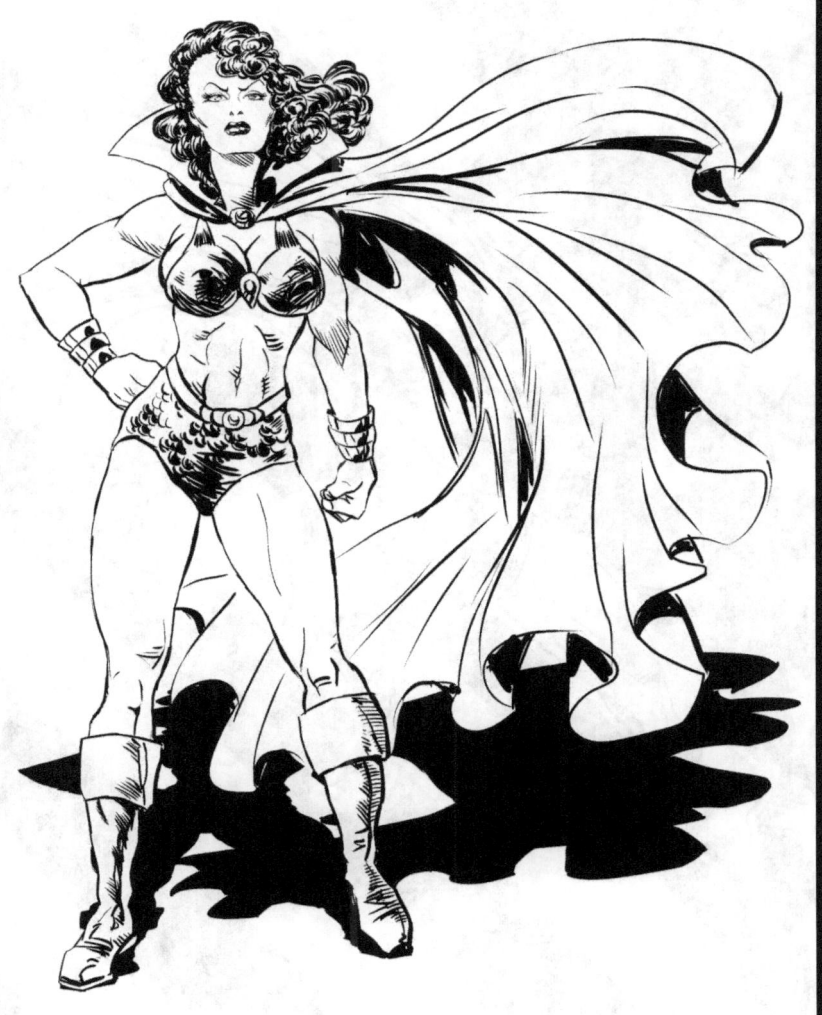

MADAME STRANGE – GREAT COMICS

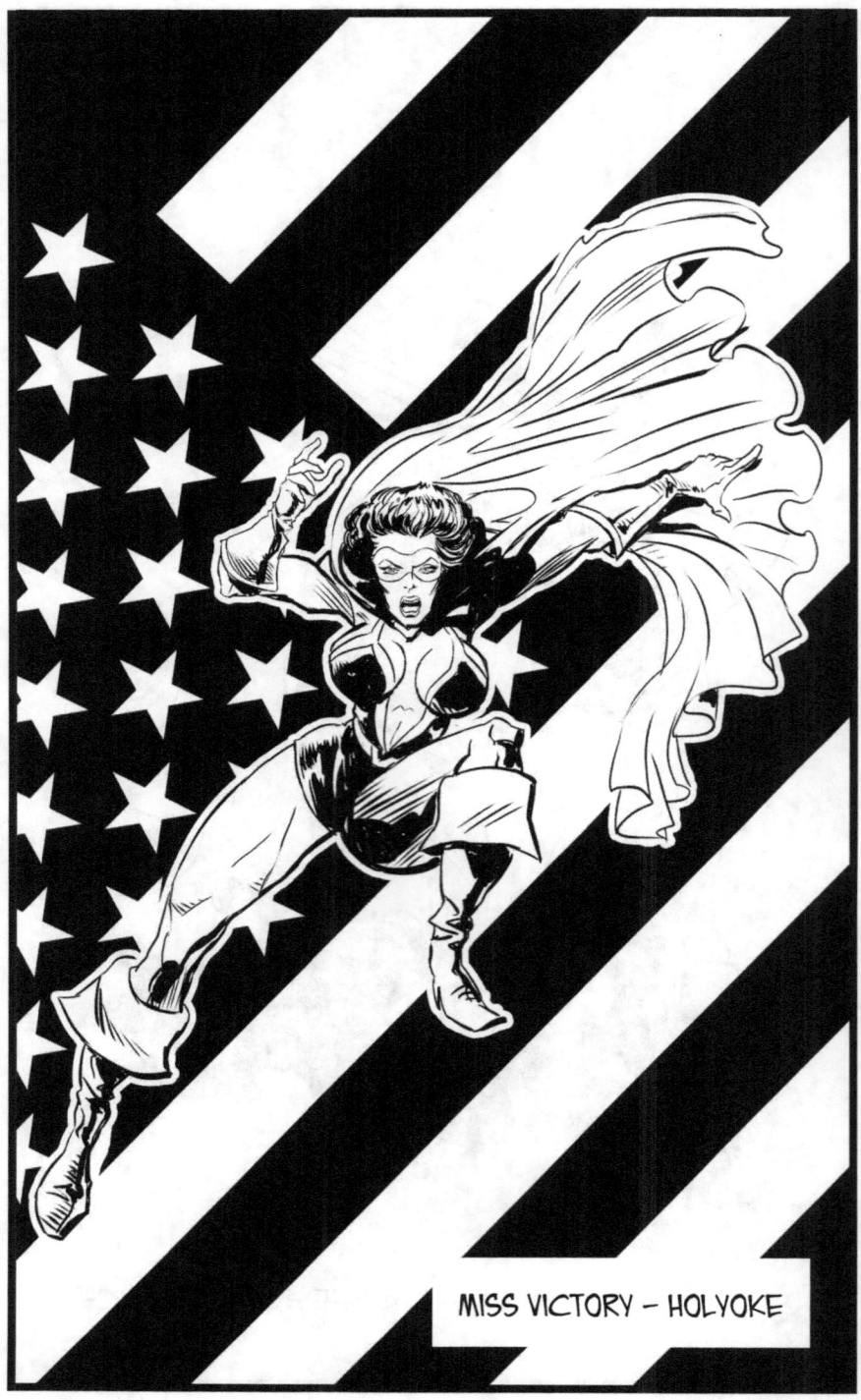

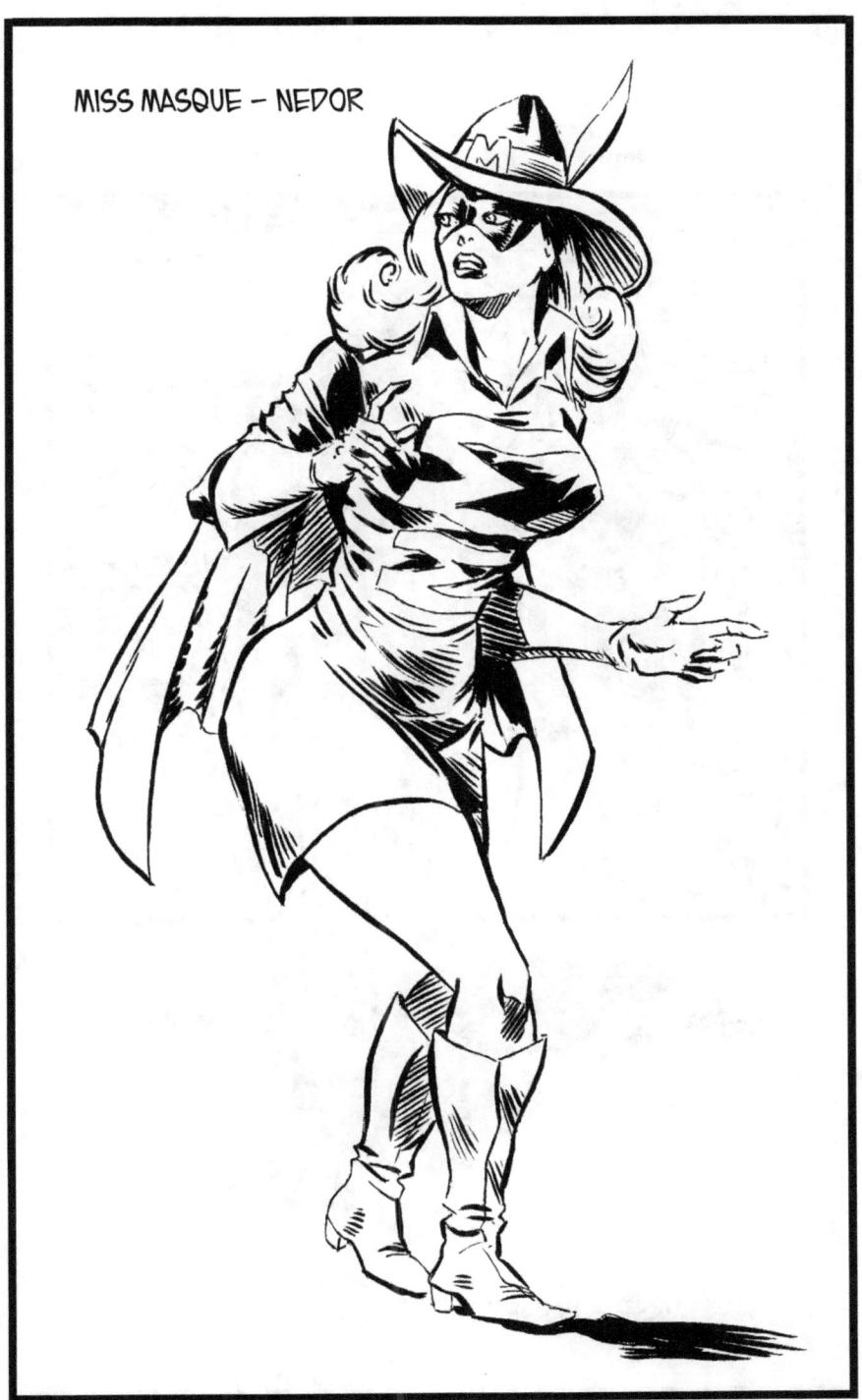

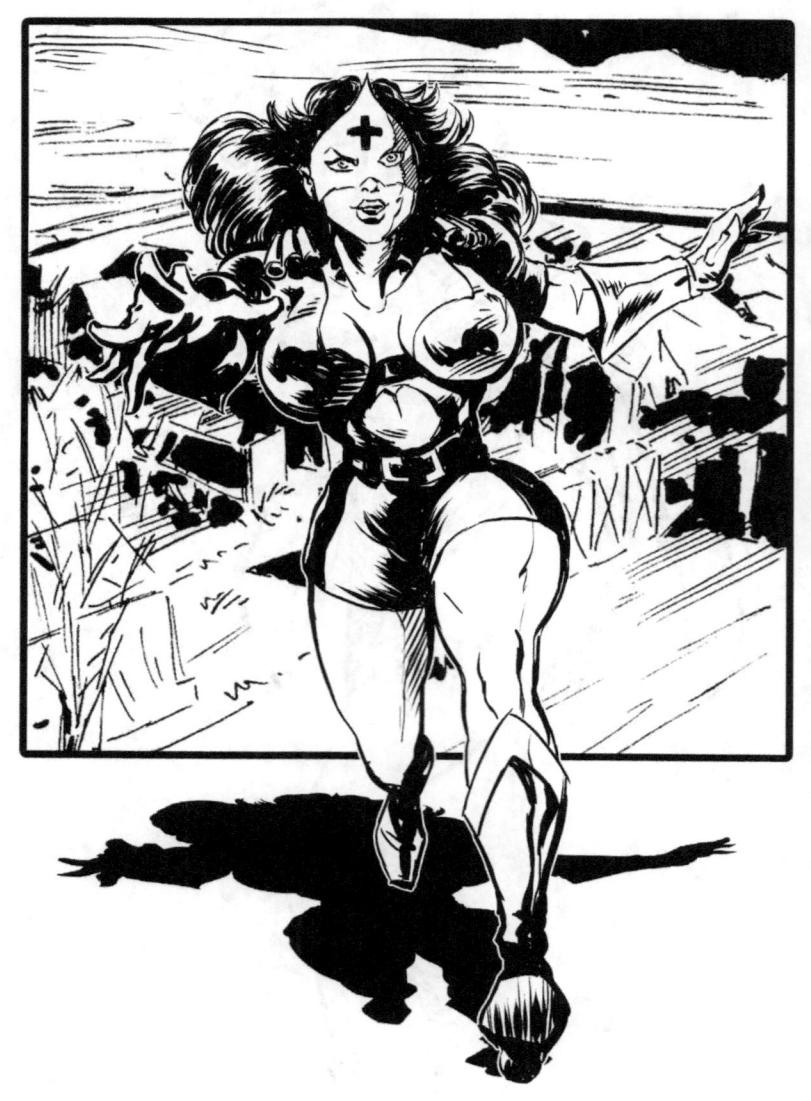

WAR NURSE - HARVEY

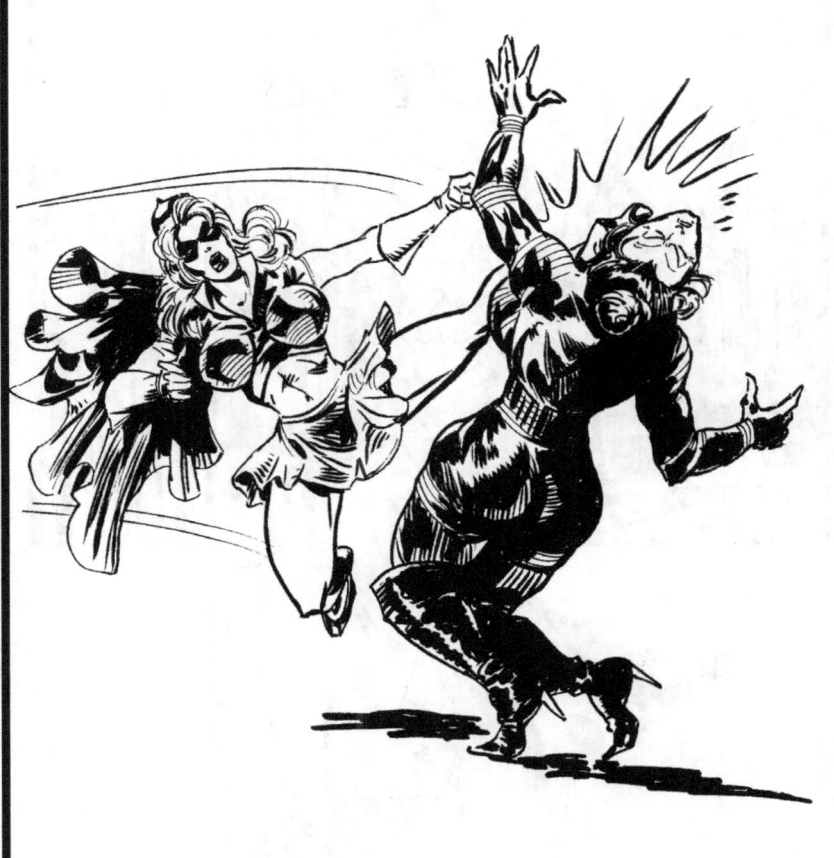

MISS MASQUE – NEDOR

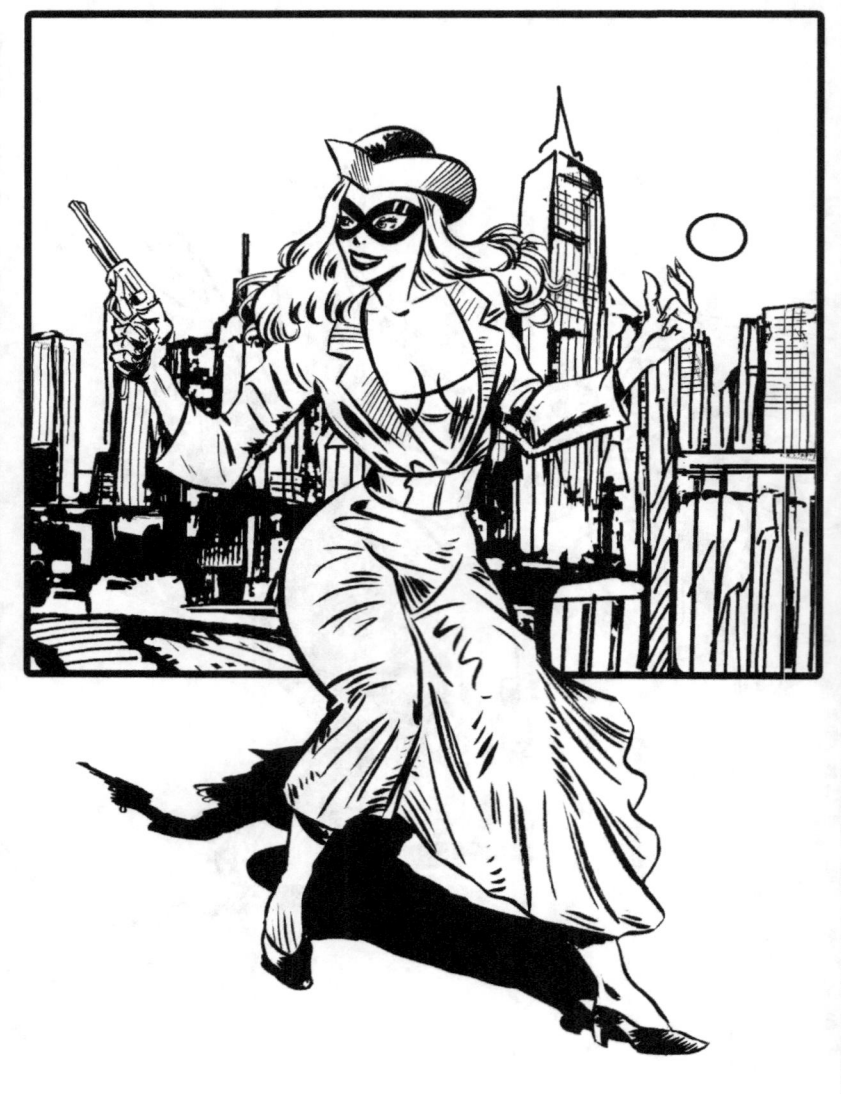

RED ANN - NEDOR

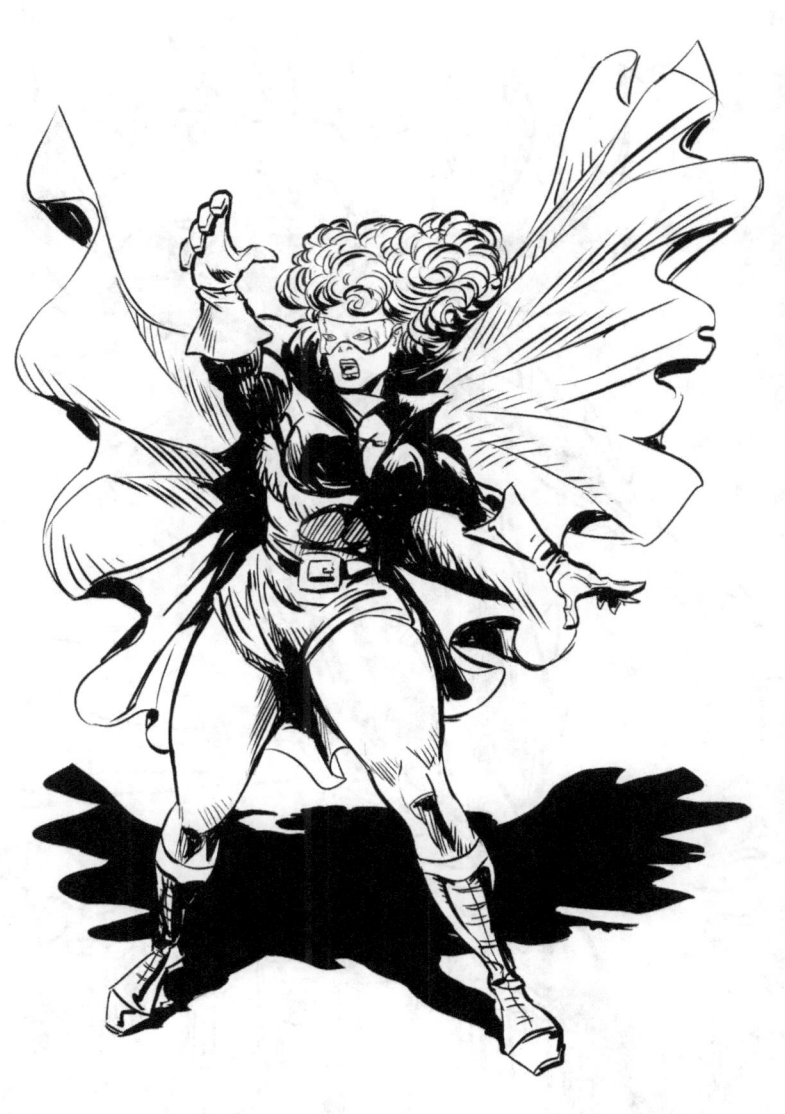

MISS VICTORY - HOLYOKE

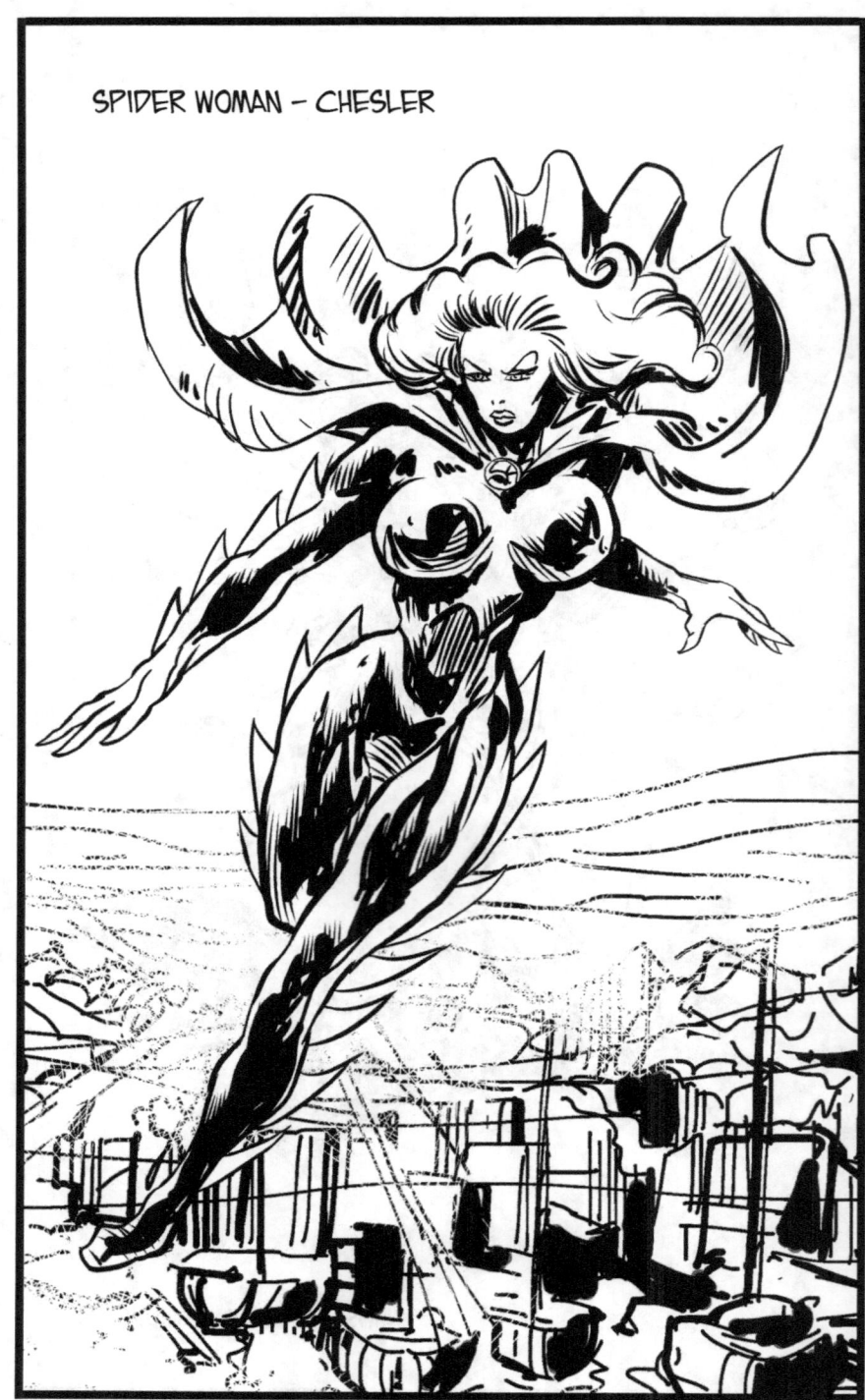
SPIDER WOMAN - CHESLER

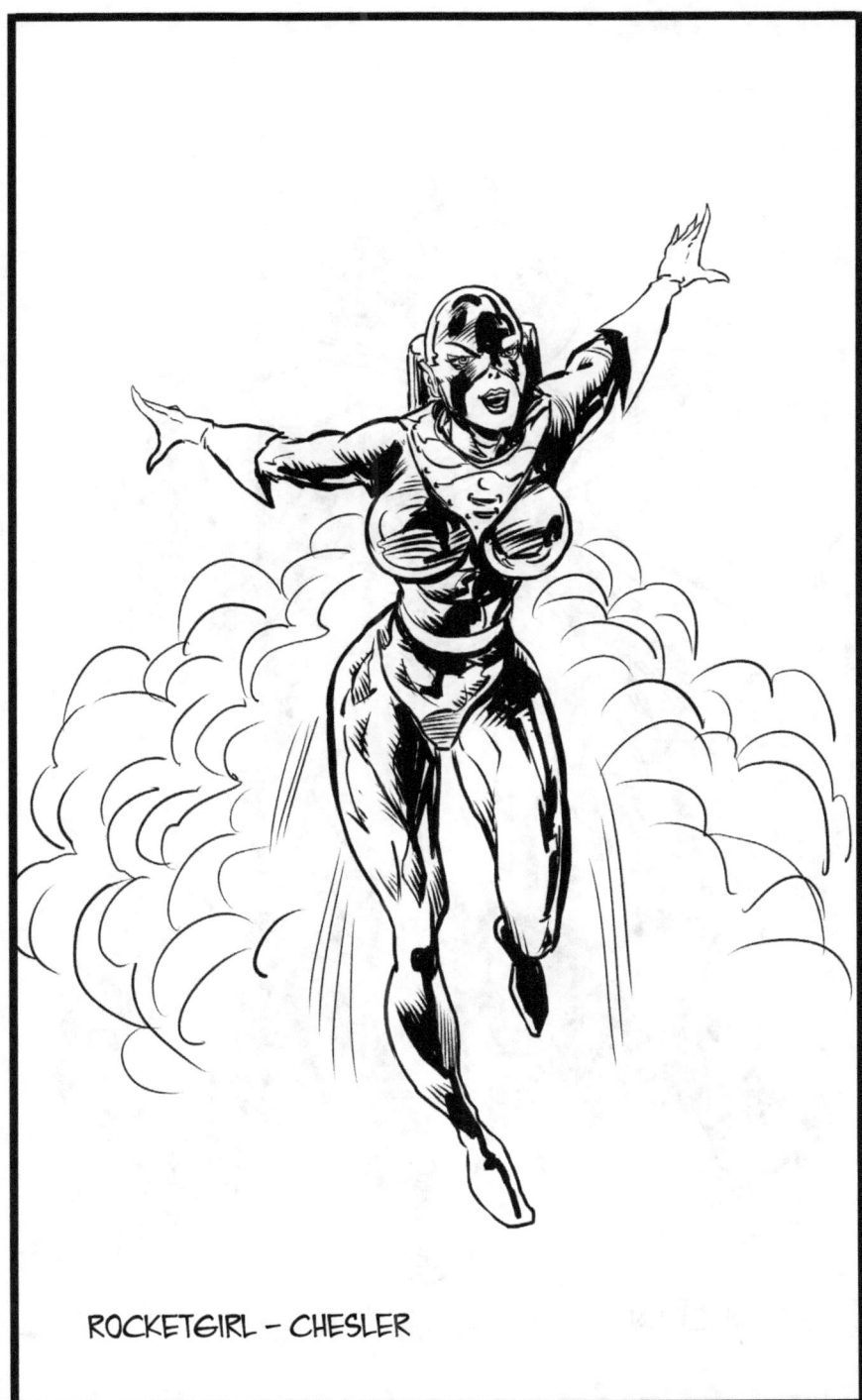

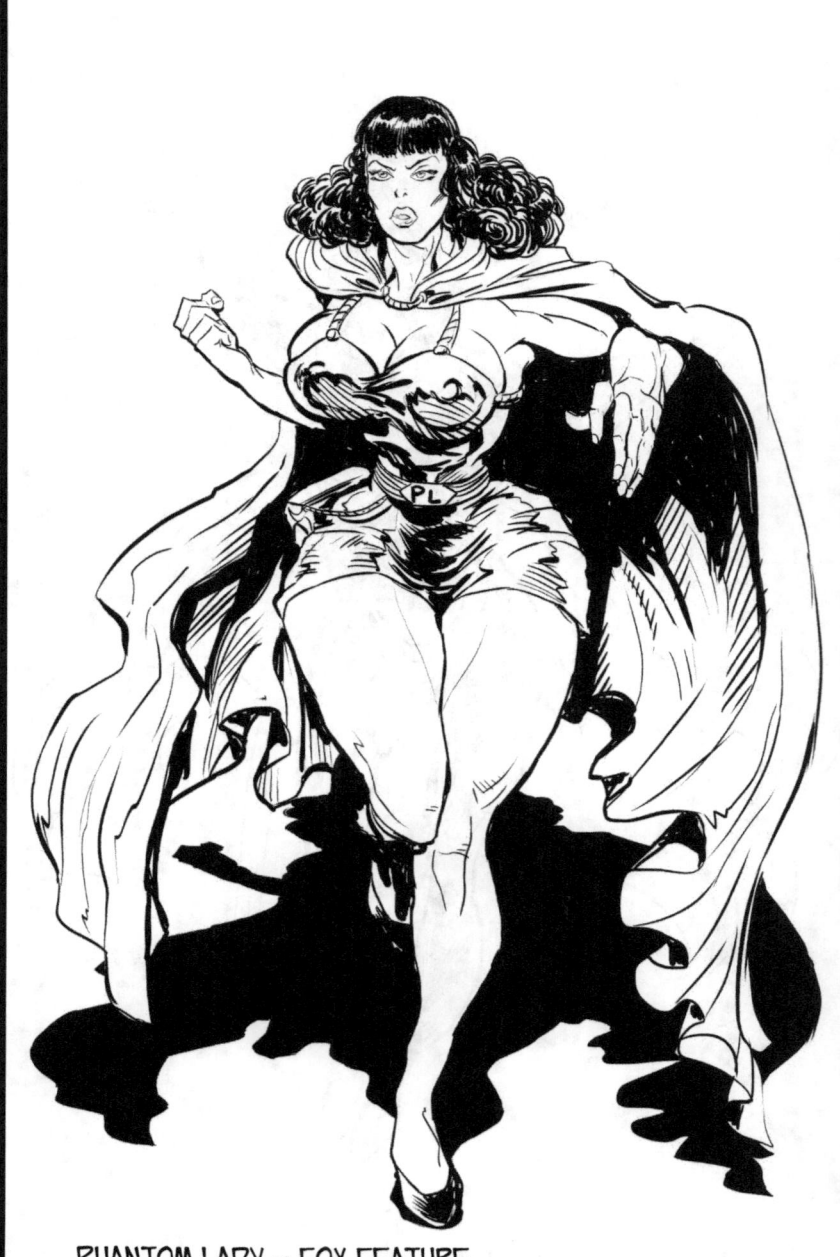

PHANTOM LADY - FOX FEATURE

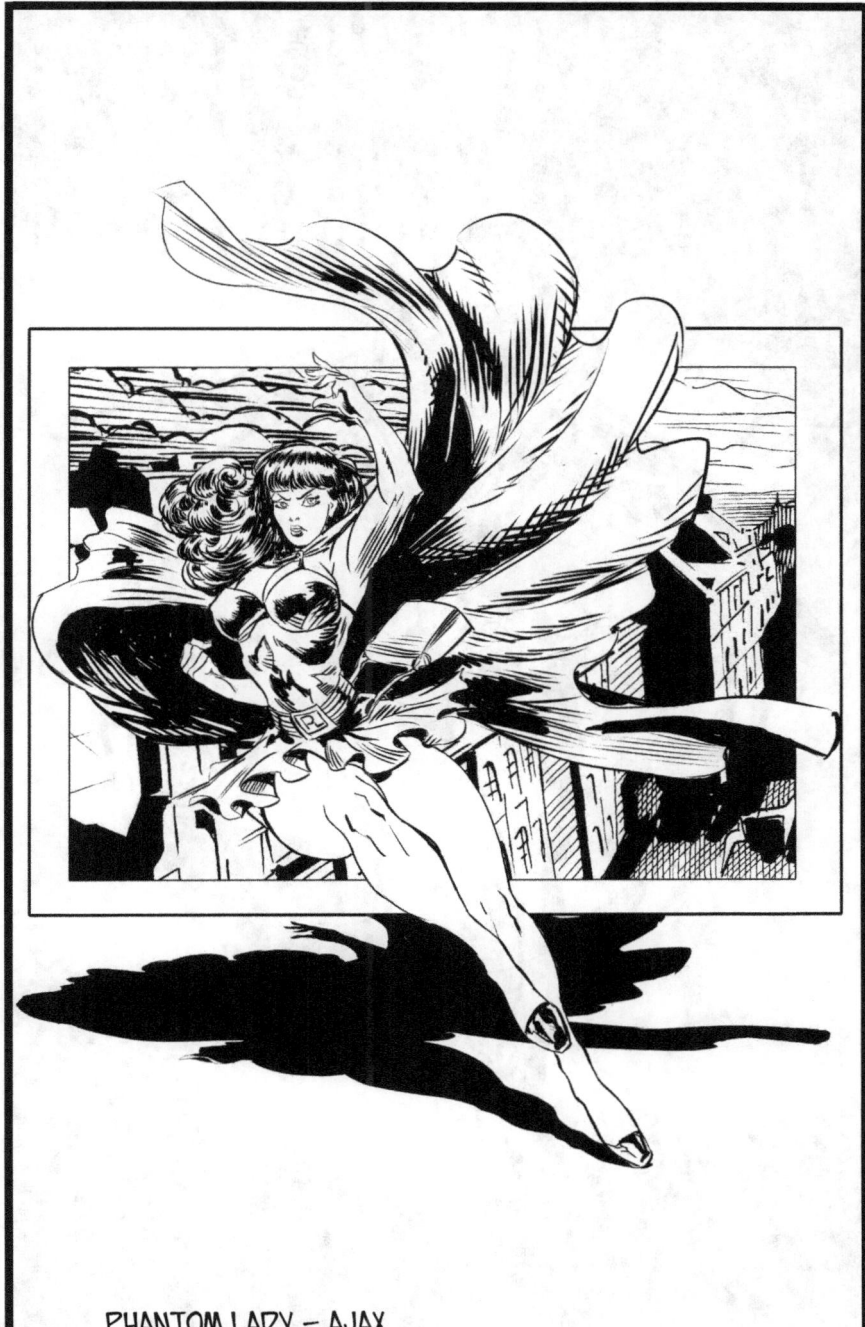

PHANTOM LADY - AJAX

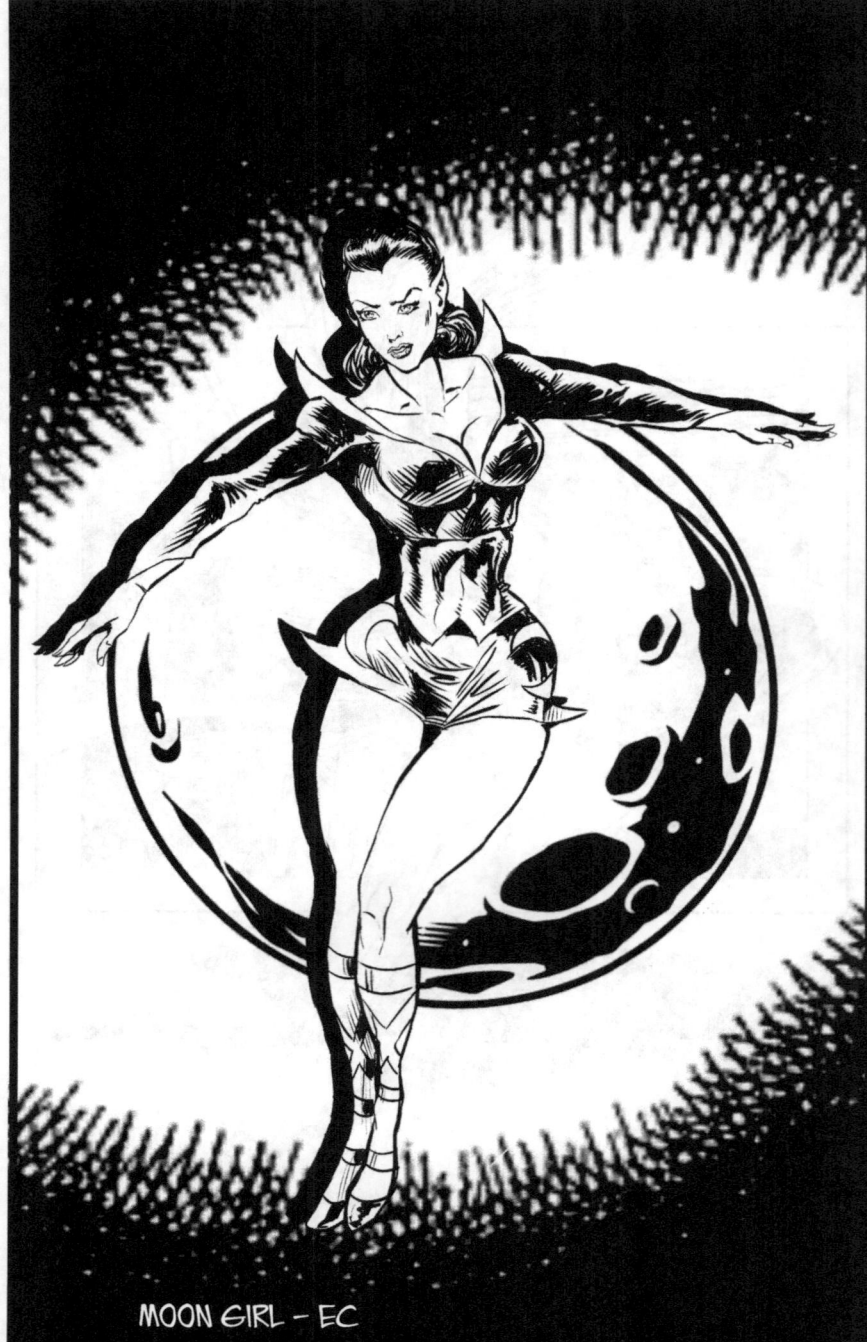

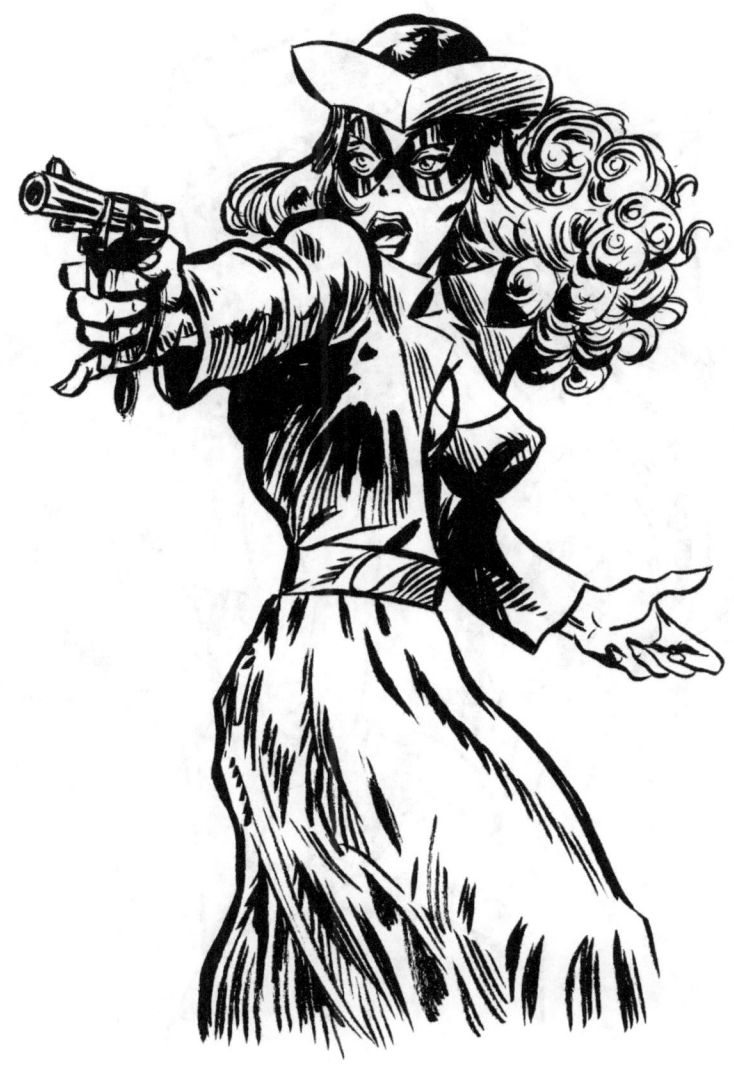

RED ANN - NEDOR

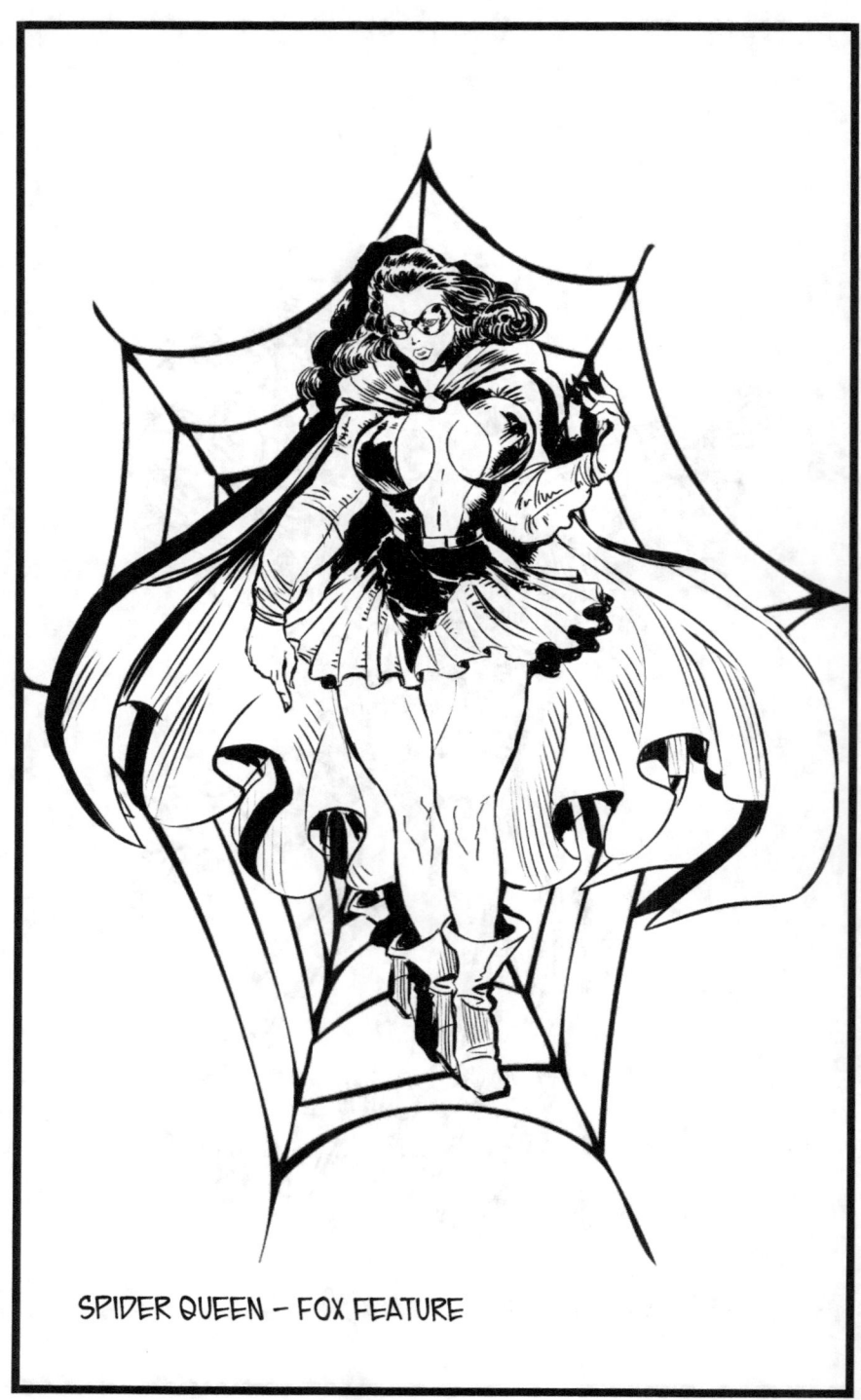

SPIDER QUEEN – FOX FEATURE

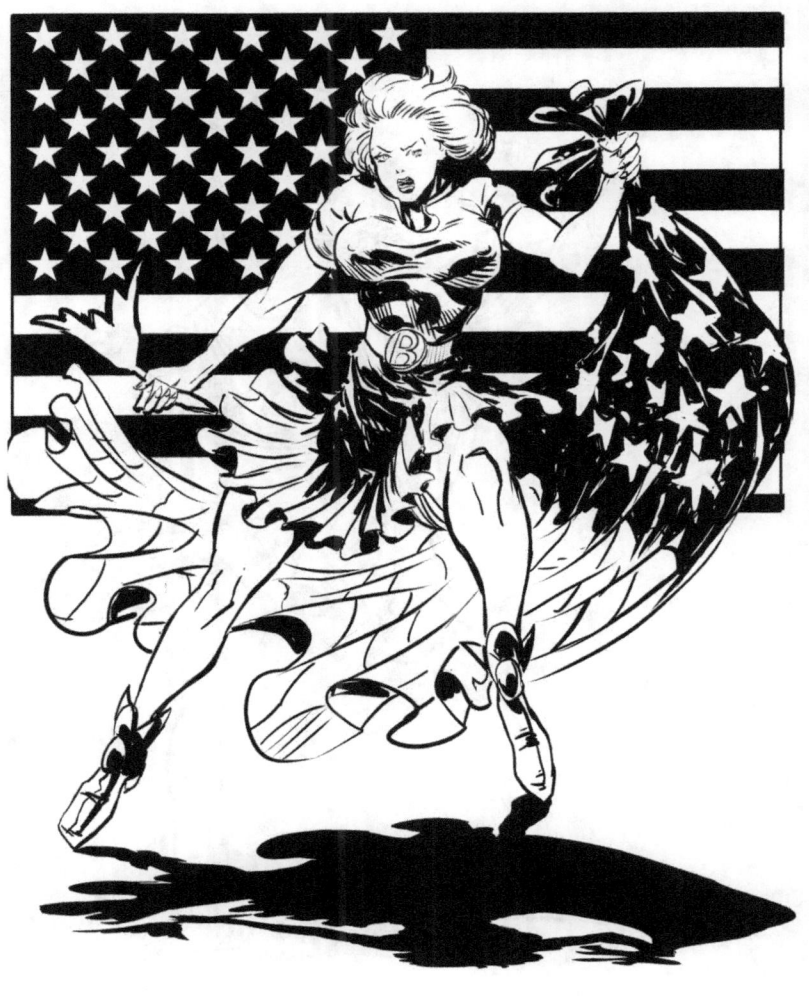

USA - QUALITY

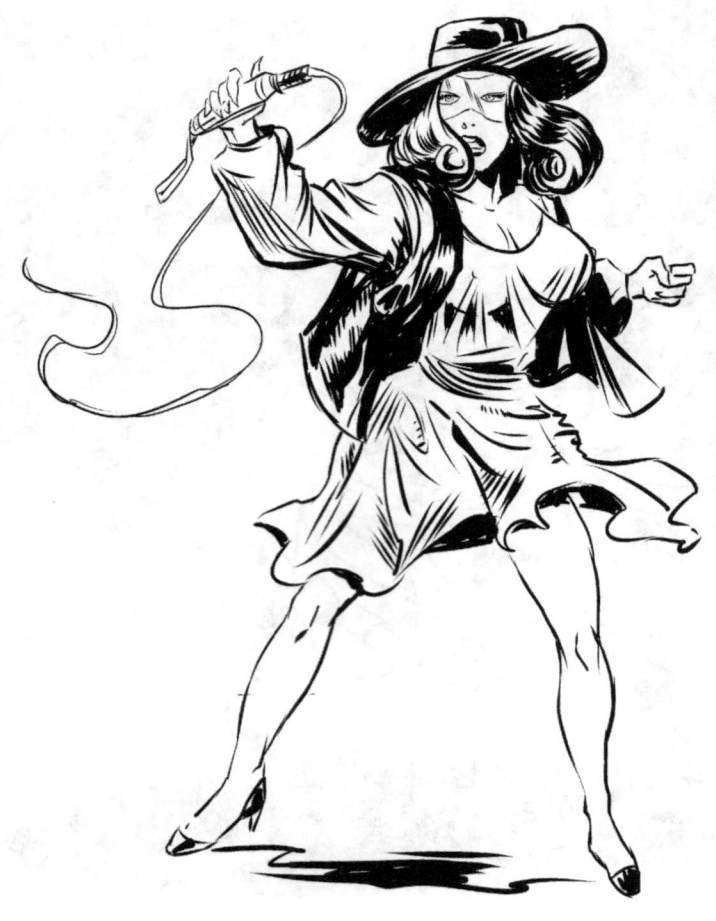

VEILED AVENGER - CHESLER

WOMAN IN RED - NEDOR

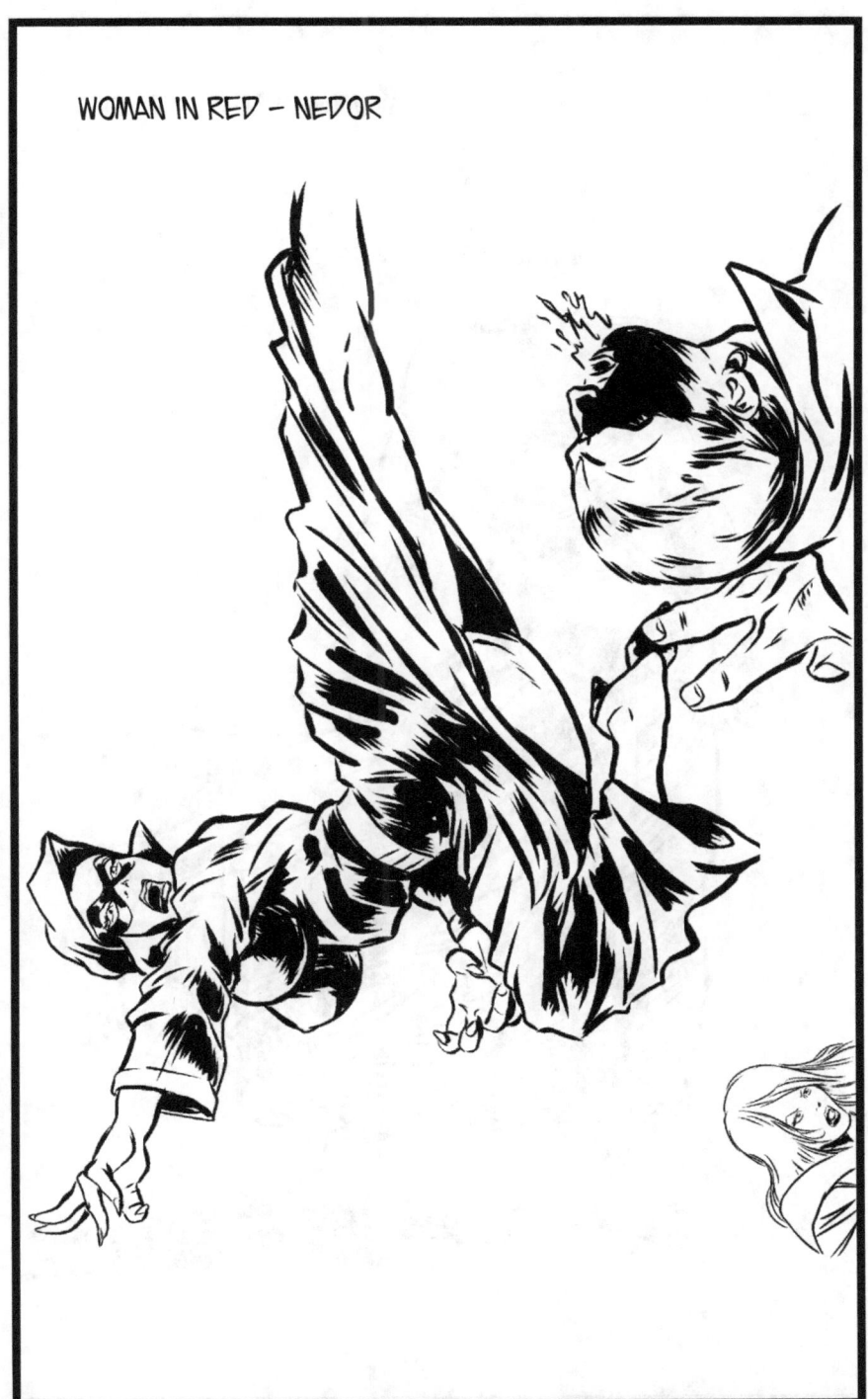

WOMAN IN RED - NEDOR

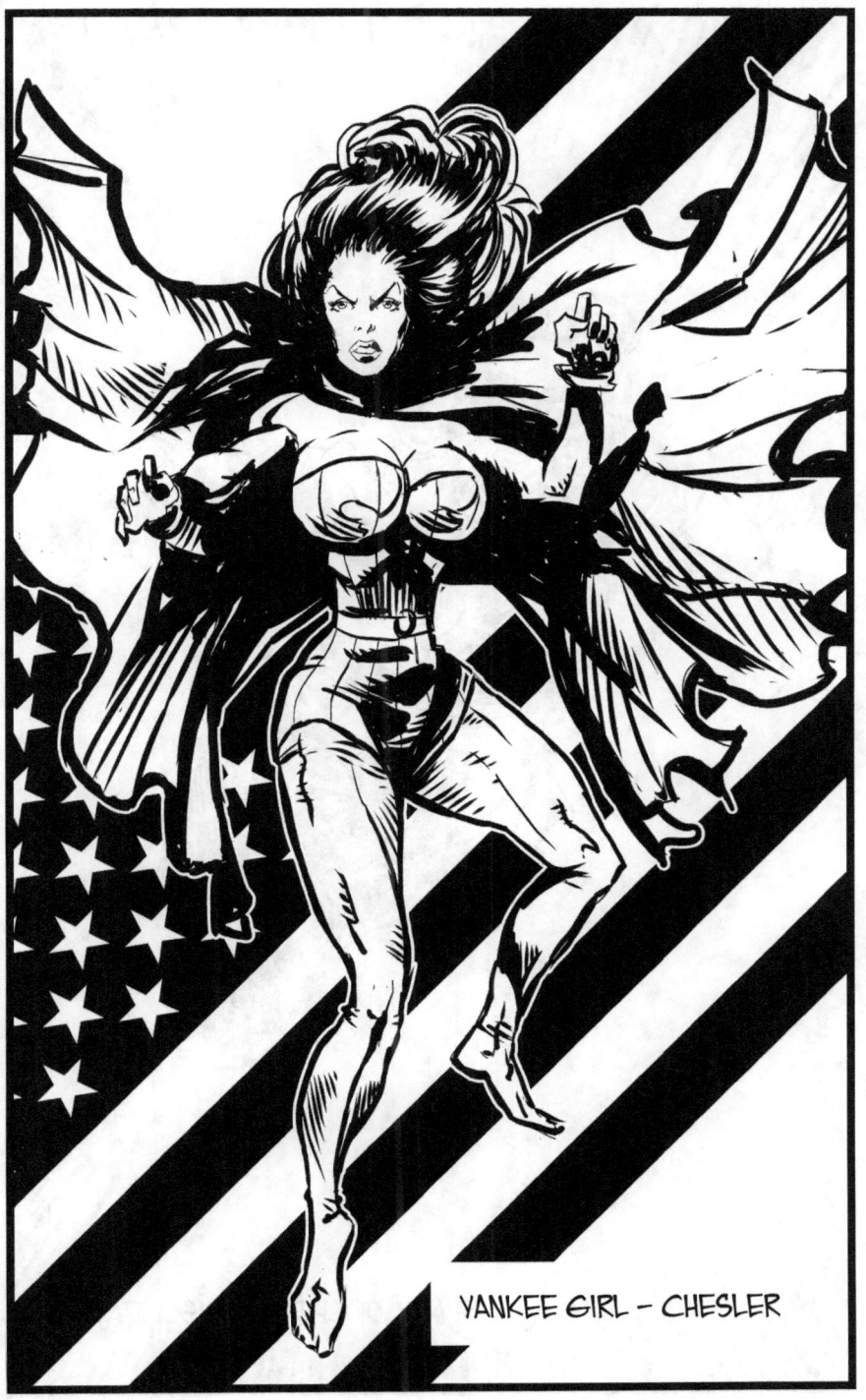

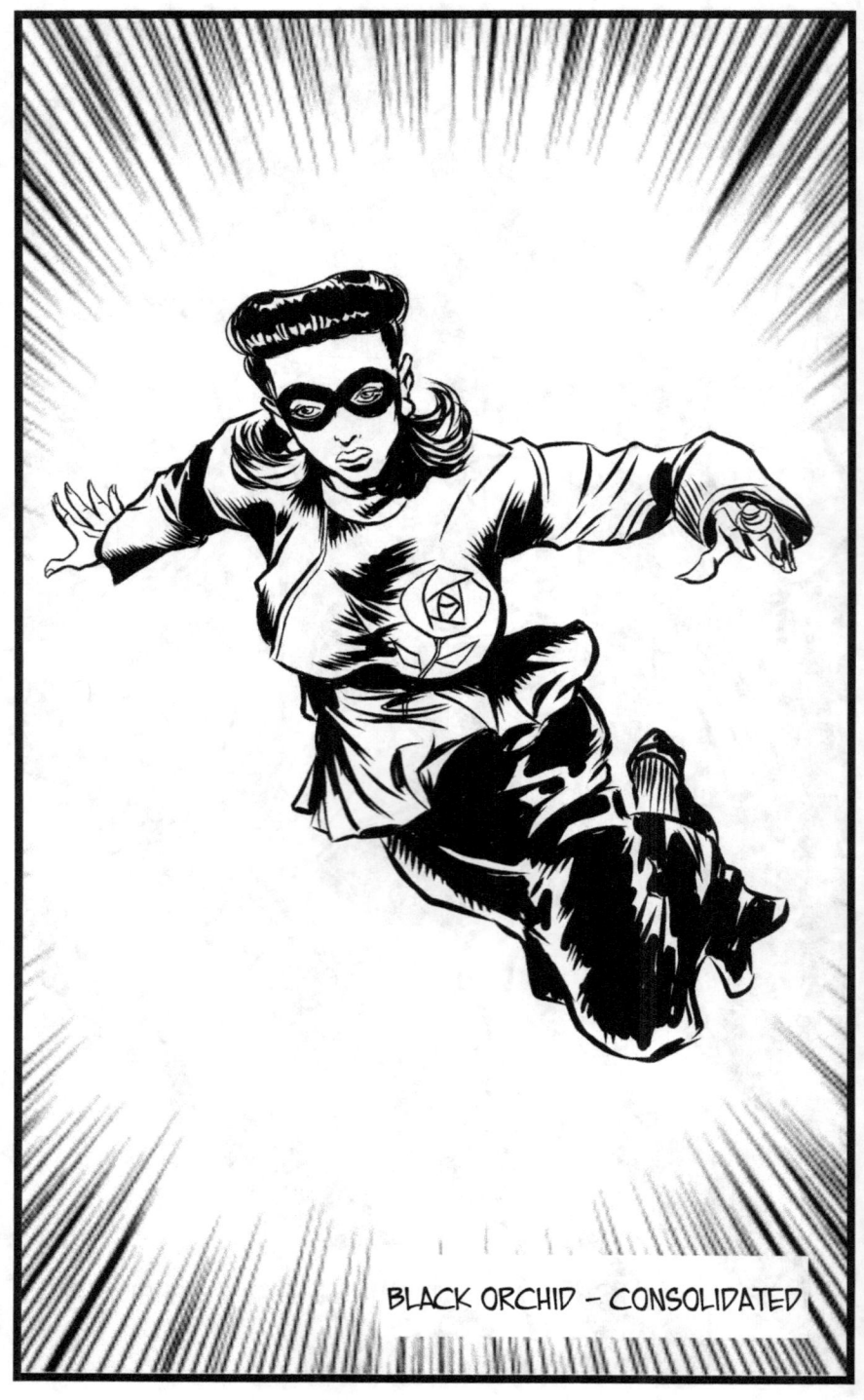

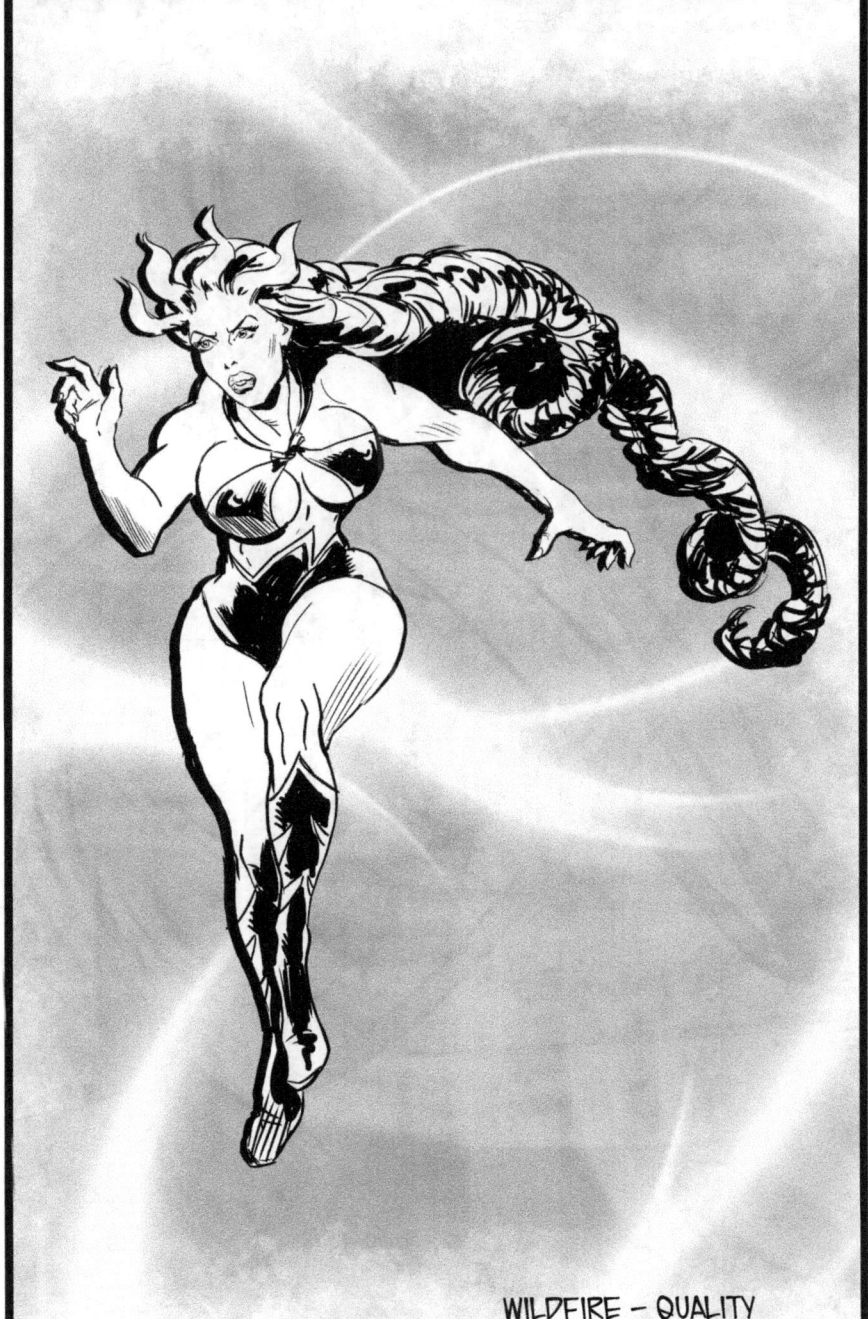

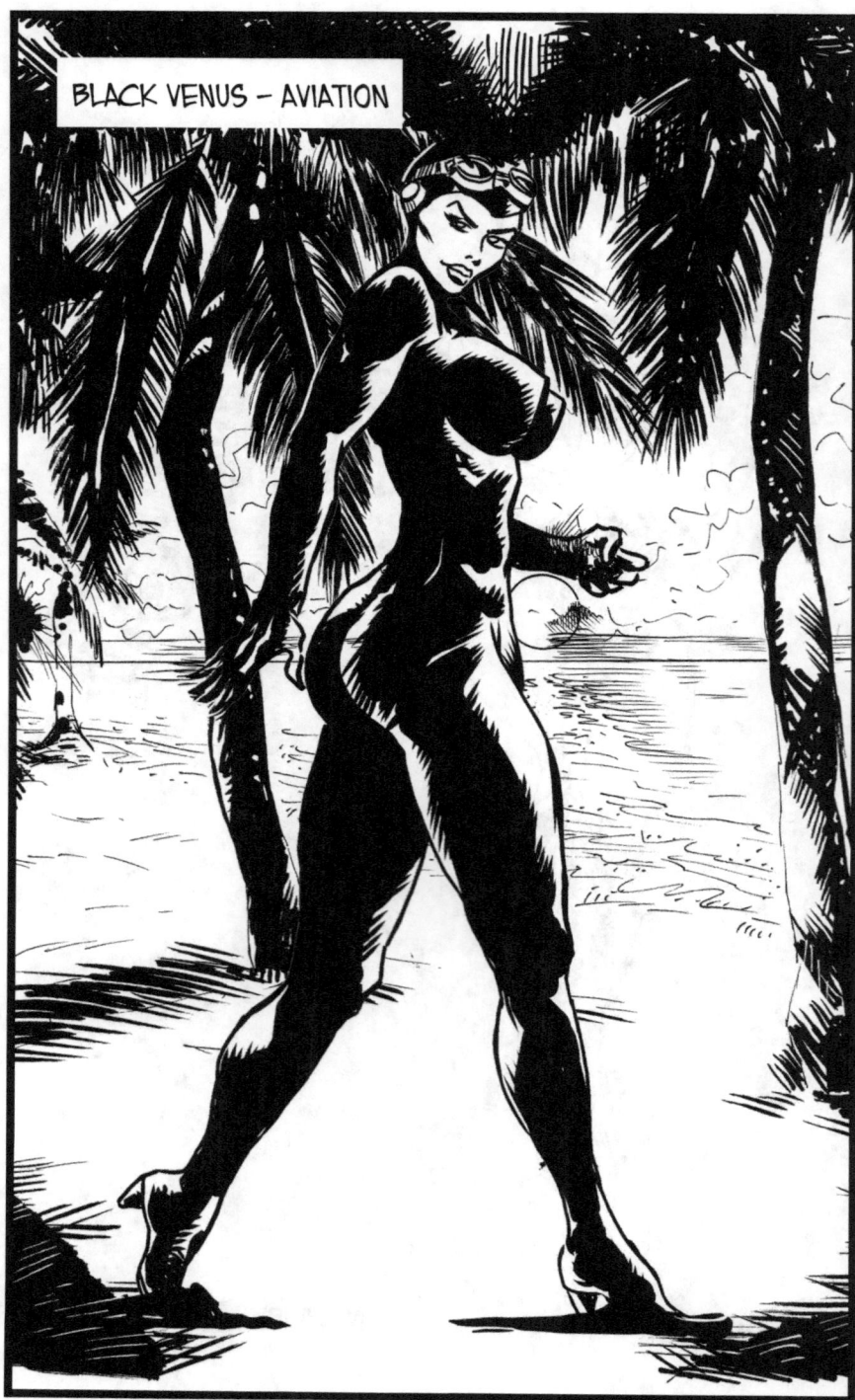

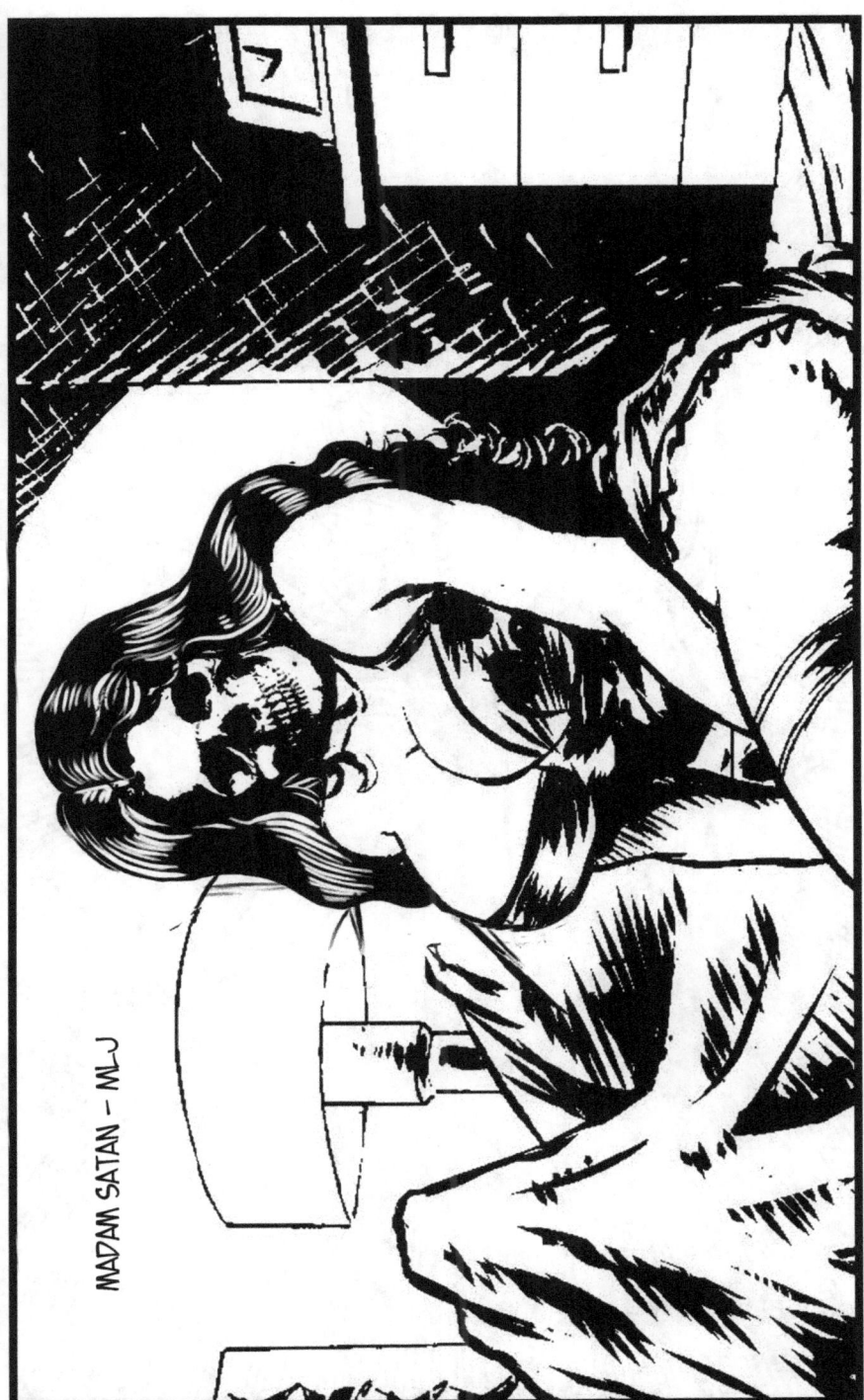

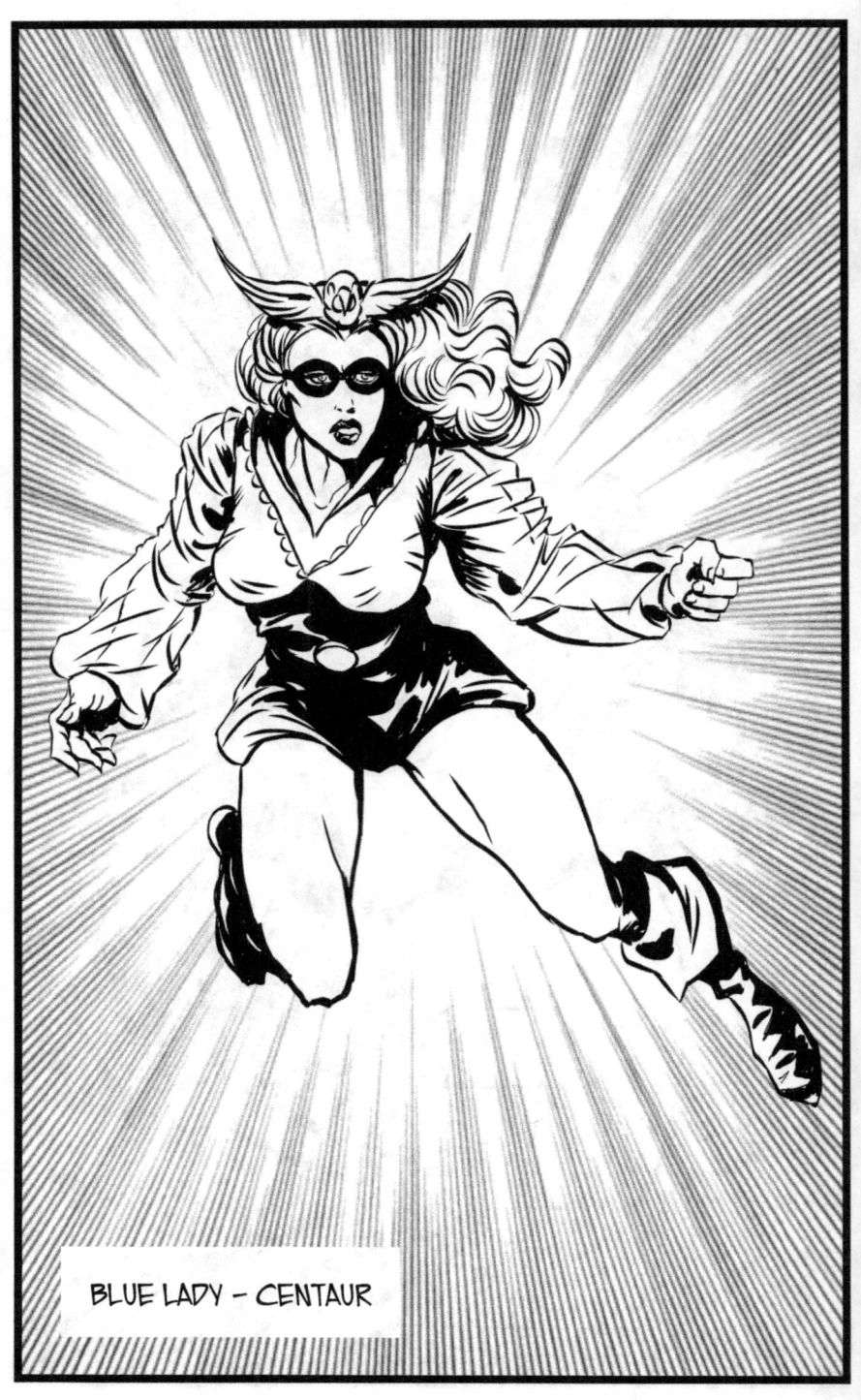

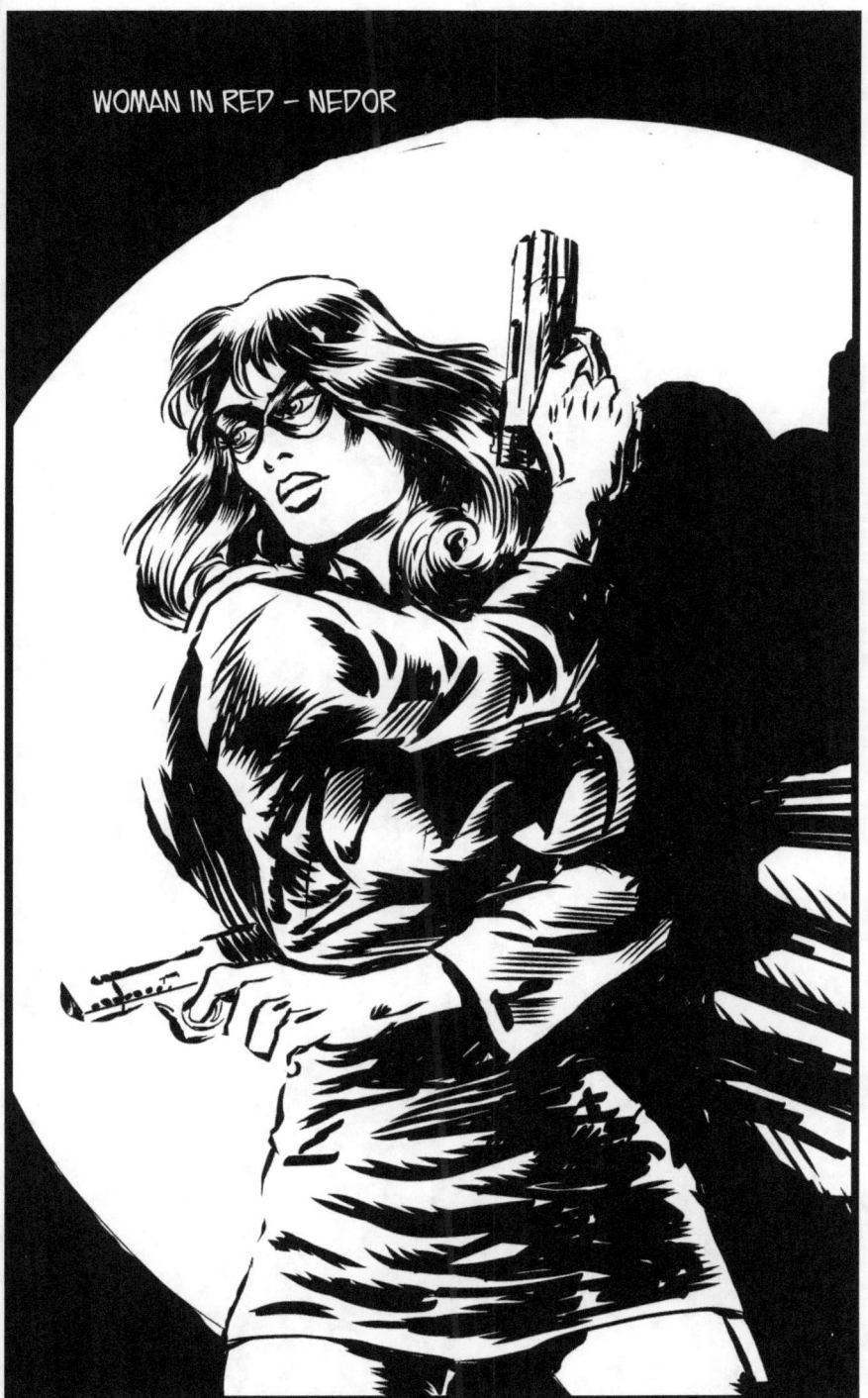

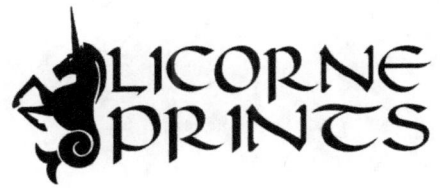

LICORNE PRINTS IS A DIVISION OF THE BMS GROUP DEDICATED TO HIGH QUALITY REPRINTS OF HISTORICAL COMIC BOOK STORIES AND NOVELS.

TO CONTACT LICORNE PRINTS DIRECTLY WRITE AT:

LICORNE@BEMYSTUDIO.COM

OR

CHECK THE LICORNE WEBSITE AT:

WWW.LICORNEPRINTS.COM

www.ingramcontent.com/pod-product-compliance
Lightning Source LLC
Chambersburg PA
CBHW070820220526
45466CB00002B/724